高等学校规划教材·语言学

Intercultural Communication
跨文化交际

主　编　杨惠英
副主编　王　娟
编　者　杨惠英　王　娟
　　　　苏小青

西北工业大学出版社

【内容简介】 本书通过介绍跨文化交际的相关概念、现象和生动案例,解读跨文化交际中的种种文化差异与冲突;阐释解决跨文化交际问题的基本知识和技能;引导学生预料和避免由于不同文化期望而产生的文化误解;锻炼学生客观认识英语国家的文化特色;提高学生跨文化交际能力和跨文化交际意识。

本书依托"陕西省社会科学基金项目""西北工业大学社科与管理研究基金项目",入选西北工业大学校级"大学英语拓展课程"系列教材,主要面向高校英语专业本科生、非英语专业本科生,以及程度相当的其他英语学习者。

图书在版编目(CIP)数据

跨文化交际/杨惠英主编. —西安:西北工业大学出版社,2016.4
高等学校规划教材. 语言学
ISBN 978-7-5612-4786-0

Ⅰ.①跨… Ⅱ.①杨… Ⅲ.①文化交流—高等学校—教材 Ⅳ.①G115

中国版本图书馆 CIP 数据核字(2016)第 058122 号

出版发行：西北工业大学出版社
通信地址：西安市友谊西路 127 号　　邮编：710072
电　　话：(029)88493844　88491757
网　　址：www.nwpup.com
印刷　者：陕西兴平市博闻印务有限公司
开　　本：787 mm×1 092 mm　　1/16
印　　张：10.75
字　　数：256 千字
版　　次：2016 年 4 月第 1 版　　2016 年 4 月第 1 次印刷
定　　价：30.00 元

前　言

　　文化上的差异会给不同文化背景的人们在相互理解与和睦共处上带来极大困扰。因此，认识跨文化交际的相关内容和现象本质，了解探究这一过程中会发生什么、怎样发生、将产生什么后果，以及如何解决与避免交际中产生的种种障碍与冲突，从而增强跨文化交际意识与提高跨文化交际能力，是21世纪英语学习者所要面临的一个时代需求，也是国际化大背景下的必然发展趋势。另外，通过与不同于本土文化的异国文化进行比较，也可以改善学生的自我认识，促使其重新审视自己的本国文化，客观认识他国文化，成为具有跨文化交际包容能力与和谐发展能力的现代人。

　　同英语国家的人们用英语进行有效交流是英语学习者的重要目的之一。然而有效的交流不仅仅是一个语言技巧问题，还涉及许多文化因素。本书的主旨是帮助英语学习者了解和学习如何正确解决在跨文化交际中因文化差异而产生的种种问题。

一、内容安排

　　本书共8个章节。

　　第1章介绍有关语言、文化和交际的基本概念及其三者之间的相互关系，以及在实际交流和交际中的案例分析。

　　第2章至第6章以"文化现象"为线索，以"案例分析"为依托，向英语学习者展示跨文化交际中一些具有代表性的跨文化交际问题，提供认识、处理这些问题以及解决这些问题的基本知识和技巧，锻炼学生的客观分析能力，培养现实交际能力，以提高跨文化交际的交流质量。

　　第7章介绍文化负载词及其在使用中需要注意的问题。

　　第8章介绍跨文化交际能力的理论认知及东西方文化的适应与相容。

二、内容特色

　　(1)突出概念的重点性和主要性，避免过于细化和烦琐，利于学生从知识层面拓展概念意义，了解跨文化交际的实质内涵。

　　(2)突出理论的简洁性和具体化，避免过于抽象和生涩，利于学生从认知层面联系生活实践，体会和理解跨文化交际的实用意义。

　　(3)突出文化现象的差异性和表现形式，避免生硬记忆，利于学生从感知层面体会文化交流的重要性和必要性。

　　(4)突出案例的生动性和趣味性，避免枯燥的知识灌输模式，利于学生从学习兴趣和学习态度上积极体会案例展示与实践经历的"近距离"，从而提高学生的跨文化交际能力。

(5) 突出拓展阅读的知识性和层次性,利于学生从不同角度学习和了解相关的背景知识和文化内涵。

本书的主编为杨惠英,副主编为王娟。全书由杨惠英、王娟和苏小青共同编写完成。

本书从讲义到正式交付书稿并出版,经历了三个学年的实践教学,不仅得到了广大师生的认可,同时采纳了众多师生的真诚意见和建议。此外,笔者还参阅了大量的专著、教材和网站资料。在此,对给予帮助的各位师生及所参阅文献的原作者表示衷心的感谢。

由于笔者的理论水平和实践经验有限,书中难免存在疏漏之处,竭诚希望得到各位专家、学者和读者的批评指正!

编　者

2016 年 3 月

CONTENTS

Chapter One   Culture and Communication 1

1.1   Understanding Culture 1
1.2   Understanding Communication 7
1.3   Relationship between Culture and Communication 10
1.4   Review Tasks 10

Chapter Two   Intercultural Communication 16

2.1   Lead-in Cases 16
2.2   What Is Intercultural Communication? 17
2.3   Intercultural Communication VS. Cross-cultural Communication ... 20
2.4   Case Discussion 20
2.5   Group Discussion 22
2.6   Further Reading 22
2.7   Review Tasks 23

Chapter Three   Daily Verbal Intercultural Communication 30

3.1   Lead-in Cases 30
3.2   Hospitality 31
3.3   Greeting 34
3.4   Concern 34
3.5   Money 36
3.6   Modesty 38
3.7   Compliments 40
3.8   Gratitude and Apology 43
3.9   "No Politeness" 45
3.10 Visiting and Parting 46
3.11 Common Topics in China and the West 51
3.12 Review Tasks 51

I

Chapter Four Non-verbal Intercultural Communication ········· 59

- 4.1 Lead-in Cases ········· 59
- 4.2 What Is Non-verbal Intercultural Communication? ········· 61
- 4.3 Functions and Significance ········· 61
- 4.4 Body Language ········· 62
- 4.5 Paralanguage ········· 69
- 4.6 Time Language ········· 71
- 4.7 Space Language ········· 74
- 4.8 Review Tasks ········· 76

Chapter Five Interpersonal Relationships ········· 81

- 5.1 Understanding Cross-gender Communication ········· 82
- 5.2 Family Relationship ········· 88
- 5.3 Friendship ········· 91
- 5.4 I/C Theory ········· 98
- 5.5 Review Tasks ········· 99

Chapter Six Naming and Addressing ········· 105

- 6.1 Cultural Differences in Naming ········· 105
- 6.2 Number of Syllables of First Names ········· 107
- 6.3 Last Sound of First Names ········· 107
- 6.4 Further Reading ········· 108
- 6.5 Cultural Differences in Forms of Address ········· 109
- 6.6 Kinship ········· 115
- 6.7 Review Tasks ········· 115

Chapter Seven Cultural-loaded Words in Communication ········· 121

- 7.1 Colors ········· 122
- 7.2 Proverbs and Idioms ········· 126
- 7.3 Cultural-loaded Idioms ········· 128
- 7.4 Numbers ········· 129
- 7.5 Taboos ········· 130
- 7.6 Review Tasks ········· 131

Chapter Eight Intercultural Communication Competence ········· 136

- 8.1 Aware of Cultural Value Differences ········· 136
- 8.2 Adapting to a New Culture ········· 141
- 8.3 Improving Intercultural Communication Competence ········· 143

8.4　An Integration of Eastern and Western Culture ················· 144
8.5　Review Tasks ·· 145

Keys to Review Tasks ·· 150

Bibliography ·· 162

Culture and Communication

> *To know another's language and not his culture is a very good way to make a fluent fool of oneself.*
> —Winston Brembeck
>
> *The greatest distance between people is not space but culture.*
> —Jamake Highwater

1.1 Understanding Culture

1.1.1 Lead-in Cases

Case one

Once upon a time a marmoset decided to leave the forest and explore the great, wide world. He traveled to the city and saw many strange and wonderful things but finally he decided to return home. Back in the forest, his friends and relatives crowded round. "Well," they cried, "What did you see?" "I saw buildings made of concrete and glass, buildings so high that they touched the sky," said the marmoset. And all his friends and relatives imagined glass branches scratching the sky.

"The buildings were full of people walking on two legs and carrying briefcases," said the marmoset. And his friends and relatives could almost see the people running along the branches with their tails wrapping firmly around their briefcases.

Questions

1. Why did they imagine people with tails?
2. What made them misrepresent the image of people?

Case two

In the TV series Genghis Khan（成吉思汗）produced by the CCTV studio, Genghis Khan, on one occasion after heavy drinking, lay down on his "bed" and said to his subordinates, "How delighted I am today! You have never known that the bed of middle China is supported on four legs. You can never imagine how comfortable it is laying on it." The subordinates racked their brains to understand. What they had in mind, however, was but a horse, or a cow, or a camel that had four legs.

Questions

1. Why were they not be able to construct in their mind the image of a bed as it is?
2. What does this story tell us about understanding between cultures?

Case three

古时候有个不学无术的人,好不容易用钱买了个县官,却不会说"官话"。他上任之后,照例要去拜访顶头上司——知府。在闲聊中知府问:

"贵县风土怎么样?"

"并没有大风,更少尘土。"

"百姓怎样?"

"白杏只有两颗,红杏不少。"

"我问的是黎庶!"

"梨树结的果实很小。"

知府动气了:"我不是问什么梨树,我是问你的小民!"

县官见知府生气,急忙站起来回答到:"卑职的小名叫狗儿。"

Questions

1. Why do you think "Zhi Fu" (prefect) was mad at "Xian Guan" (county magistrate)?
2. What caused the difficulties in the communication?

Case four

In Hong Kong, a Chinese policeman A goes to his British superior B and asks for leave to take his mother to the hospital.

A：Sir?

B：Yes, what is it?

A：My mother is not very well, sir.

B：So?

A：She has to go into hospital, sir.

B：Well, get on with it. What do you want?

A：On Thursday, sir.

B: Bloody hell, man (很生气). What do you want?
A: Nothing, sir.

Questions

1. Why does B turn out to be angry at A in the conversation?
2. What caused the conflict between the two speakers?

1.1.2　What is Culture?

It is true that as human beings we share commonalities. But there are many differences that distinguish us from one another. It is just these differences that make the world diverse. However, this is where miscommunication, misunderstanding and even conflict may occur. What naturally follows is that we need to know something of other cultures as well as our own if we hope to achieve development and harmony in the world.

What is Chinese about a Chinese? Or American about an American? Australian about an Australian? German about a German? French about a French? ...

In answering such questions, we would usually give a list of traits, certain ideas, certain ways of behaving, or even certain products that would, in general, be associated with the concept of "a Chinese" or "an American" or "an Australian", etc. We would, in fact, describe a culture. Members of a particular culture have certain things in common, e.g. certain customs, certain gestures and certain foods. They may also share distinctive artifacts, distinctive art, distinctive music, literature and folk stories.

The way of regarding culture as an observable pattern of behavior is a useful one but has its limitations. One question that tends to remain unanswered is, "what leads members of a particular culture to agree that certain behaviors have certain meanings." For example, how does an Australian man know that when another man approaches him in a pub, pats him on the back and says "How ya goin' you ol' bastard", he is expressing friendship and intimacy.

Members of a culture share patterns of behavior, and they also share models of how the world works and how its myriads of aspects relate to each other. These models are crucial not only in deciding how to interpret what is going on in any given situation, but also in molding actions and responses. In other words, culture can be seen as shared knowledge, what people need to know in order to act appropriately in a given culture.

However, it is also important to remember that culture is not a static entity. It is constantly changing and evolving under the impact of and as a result of contact with other cultures. Changes in certain aspects of culture, especially in the area of behavior and customs, can occur rapidly. Changes in underlying values, e.g. in ways of looking at the world, tend to be much slower.

What we see about culture is just the tip of the iceberg; the majority of it is intangible, beyond sight.

Based on the above Questions, we need to clarify the definition of culture in a deeper sense. Semantically, the word "culture" stems from the Latin "colere", translatable as "to build on, to cultivate, and to foster". This term, referring to something constructed willingly by men, composes the opposite of "nature" that is given in itself. According to Hofstede, culture is the collective programming of the mind which distinguishes the members of one category of people from another. (Hofstede, 1991)

Culture is a very extensive concept, it is very difficult to define it strictly and accurately because culture involves too much. We may use some metaphors to symbolize culture and may understand what culture is like through the following images: 1) culture is like an iceberg; 2) culture is like the water a fish swims in; 3) culture is our software.

First of all, culture is like an iceberg (see Figure 1.1), as mentioned above. What we can see is only a very small part of the whole culture, just like the part of the iceberg in the sea. This tangible part includes food, dress, paintings, architecture, statues, etc. The most part of culture, however, just like the iceberg which is hidden under the sea, exists but cannot be easily perceived such as views, ideas, attitudes, love, hatred, customs, habits and so on.

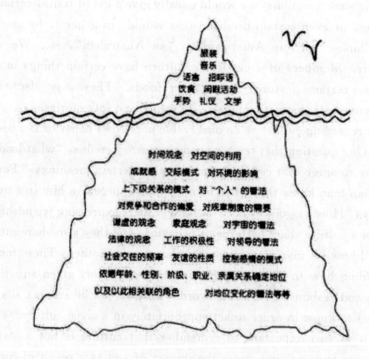

Figure 1.1

Second, culture is like the water a fish swims in. Human beings are living in a certain culture but even without realizing it, as a fish never finds out what it is like about the water it swims in. We are not aware of culture, because we are too familiar with it, and it has just become part of our living surroundings, or even part of us.

Last but not the least, culture is our software. Taking computer software for example, although hardware is important, software is the fundamental factor that determines how well it serves the development of human society. High technology which is applied into computer software is the key to human civilization, and the same to culture.

In a word, culture generally refers to a shared background (e.g. national, ethnic, religious) resulting from a common language and communication style, customs, beliefs, attitudes, and values. It includes the informal and often hidden patterns of human interactions, expressions, and viewpoints that people in one culture share.

1.1.3 Characteristics of Culture

1. Culture is learned, not hereditary

The needs that we are born with are basic needs such as food, clothing and shelter. Humans need food, but what to eat, when, where and how to eat is learned. That's why we Chinese use chopsticks while Westerners prefer knives and forks; we like rice while Americans prefer bread. We learn our culture in many ways and from a variety of sources, either consciously or unconsciously. One way is by means of proverbs that offer in a vivid way an important set of instructions for members to follow.

2. Culture is transmitted from generation to generation

Without the advantage of knowledge from those who lived before us, we would not have culture. A culture is but one link in the whole chain of generations, some of which have become history and some of which are in transition.

3. Culture is dynamic

Cultures, once formed, are stable, but are at the same time changing with the development of human society. Contact, by its nature, brings change. Cultures also change through several mechanisms: innovation, diffusion, and acculturation being the most common. Although many aspects of culture are subject to change, the deep structure of a culture resists major alterations. That is, changes in dress, food, transportation, housing, etc. are likely to occur very quickly.

However, values associated with ethics and morals, work and leisure, definitions of freedom, the importance of the past, religious practices, and attitudes toward gender and age are so deeply embedded in a culture that they persist generation after generation.

4. Most of culture is hidden, like the part of the iceberg under water

It's difficult to study culture because most of what we call culture is of an intangible nature and cannot be seen. That is to say, most of culture exists in the subconscious mind of people, who therefore aren't aware of the fact that their actions are governed by their own culture, or cultural rules.

5. Values are the core of culture

Cultures are mainly differentiated from others by way of different values people hold.

Many of these differences can be seen from what people do. For example, Western people celebrate Christmas; people in East Asia celebrate Spring Festival. People like to hear compliments and praise, but people from different cultures respond differently to the same compliments and praises.

6. Cultural elements are integrated

They are closely linked as if in a complex chain like system. You touch a culture in one place and everything else is affected. A good example of this is the Opening and Reforming in China, which has brought huge changes not only in the areas of the economy, but also in many other sectors including politics, education and so on.

7. Culture is ethnocentric

Practices that differ from one's own are usually considered strange, even abnormal or barbarous. This is the manifestation of ethnocentrism. Ethnocentrism, the belief that one's culture is primary to all explanations of reality, is usually learned at the unconscious level. It often leads to a negative evaluation of another culture's ways of doing things, because a logic extension of ethnocentrism is that our way is the right way.

Questions

1. How much do you know about the following holidays? Christmas Day; Saint Valentine's Day; April Fools' Day; Mother's Day.

2. Many overseas Chinese have lived abroad for many years. Most of their customs and behavior have been assimilated into the local cultures with their underlying values and worldviews still Chinese. How would you comment on this? Illustrate your opinions with examples.

1.1.4 Basic Functions of Culture

Dressler and Carns (1969) offer the followings as the functions of culture:

(1) Culture enables us to communicate with others through a language that we have learned and that we share in common.

(2) Culture makes it possible to anticipate how others in our society are likely to respond to our actions.

(3) Culture gives us standards for distinguishing between what is considered right or wrong, beautiful and ugly, reasonable and unreasonable, tragic and humorous, safe and dangerous.

(4) Culture provides the knowledge and skill necessary for meeting sustenance needs.

(5) Culture enables us to identify with—that is, include ourselves in the same category with—other people of similar background.

Chapter One
Culture and Communication

1.2 Understanding Communication

1.2.1 Lead-in Cases

Case one

Teacher: Who can guess what it is a small animal with four legs that people often keep as a pet and can catch mice easily?

A Chinese student: It is called "mao" in Chinese.
A French student: It is called "Chat" in French.
A Japanese student: "Neiko" in Japanese.
A Spanish student: "Gato" in Spanish.
A German student: "Katze" in German.
A Russian student: "Kosta" in Russian.

Questions

1. Do we use the same word to symbolize a certain object when we communicate with those speaking different languages?
2. What kind of process is involved in communication?

Case two

Study the following communication situations and work in groups to identify as many types of communication as you can. Then try to figure out the criteria on which you base your classification.

- An orator delivers a speech to a large gathering.
- You complain to your instructor about your course credits through telephone.
- Two blind people exchange ideas in Braille.
- A farmer gives instructions to his plough working cow.
- A programmer issues commands to a computer.
- Tom talks to himself while brandishing his toy gun.
- An archaeologist is deciphering a mysterious sign on the recently unearthed pot.
- An Arabic traveler talks you to in Arabic.
- A hen clucks to her chicks.
- My washing machine receives commands from the built-in computer.

1.2.2 What is Communication?

Communication is central to our existence. Our experiences tell us that communication is closely connected with our everyday life; without it we can hardly survive. Communication, the basis of all human contact, is as old as humankind. Today it has become even more important. Some people believe that information means power and money. Whoever has information has power, and hence has control over those less informed. Whether you agree or not, it indicates that we have to take communication very seriously.

It is through communication that we learn who we are, and what the world around us is like. To a large extent, our identity as both individual and cultural being is shaped through communication. Through this, we explore the world around us, and establish bounds, networks, and relationships with other people. Communication permits us to express our thoughts and feelings to others, and to satisfy our emotional and material needs. As we learn to communicate better, we begin to achieve some measure of control over events that affect us and those around us.

In a simple word, communication is a dynamic, systematic process in which meanings are created and reflected in human interaction with symbols.

1.2.3 Characteristics of Communication

1. Communication is dynamic

It's more like a motion picture than a single snapshot. When we communicate, we interact with each other. When we don't like an idea, we replace it with another. We sometimes even shift topics in the middle of a sentence.

2. Communication is irreversible

Once a person has said and another has received and decoded the massage, the original sender cannot take it back. Once a communication event takes place, it is done. Even if you can experience a similar event, it cannot be an identical one.

3. Communication is systemic

It is part of a large system. We send and receive messages not in isolation, but in a specific setting or context. The nature of communication depends on this context. The elements of this system include: 1) the place or location; 2) the occasion; 3) the time when the communication takes place; 4) the number of participants.

4. Communication is meaning loaded

Humans are meaning-seeking creatures. Throughout our lifetime we have accumulated various meanings as the outside world has sent us trillions of messages. These meanings are stored somewhere in our brains for us to retrieve and employ. In each communication event participants attribute to a behavior. Then meaning exchange is more obvious.

5. Communication is symbolic

Humans are symbol-making creatures. We are able to generate, receive, store, and control symbols. Human symbolic communication is man's alone. We have at hand very different types of symbols to conduct communication with: sound, light, a statue, Braille, or a painting etc. that represents something else. Our words and actions are other sets of symbols (very important ones) through which we convey our messages, ideas and feelings to other people.

6. Communication is self-reflective

Just as we use symbols to reflect what is going on around us, we also use them to reflect ourselves. This unique ability enables us to be participants and observers simultaneously: we can watch, evaluate, and alter our performances as communicators in communication events.

7. Communication has a consequence

That is to say, when we receive a message, something happens to us. For instance, when someone asks you how to go to Dean's office, your natural response is to say, "It's over there." And you might even point to that direction. Moreover, you surely feel happy on hearing "You look great!" So regardless of the content of the message, it should be clear that the act of communication produces changes in people.

1.2.4 Types of Communication

Ways of classifying communication could be broadly split into two kinds, based on communicating forms and communicator types respectively.

In terms of communicating forms, it includes verbal and non-verbal communication. Verbal communication is when language is used as methods of conversation involving several individuals. It could be by spoken or written words. Scientific study has discovered that, on the average, an individual devotes 10 up to 11 hours each day for verbal communication. These processes include speaking, hearing, writing or reading. Some typical types of verbal communication include speeches, letters, conversations, magazines, newspapers, cassettes both video and audio, telephone conversations and so on.

According to communicator types, communication can be classified as:

(1) International communication: A Japanese Prime Minister communicates with an American President.

(2) Interracial communication: An Afro-American interacts with a White American.

(3) Inter-ethnic communication: A Tibetan communicates with a Han Chinese.

(4) Inter-regional communication: In China a northerner interacts with a southerner.

1.3 Relationship between Culture and Communication

Communication permeates our life, and our life is guided by our cultures. Communication itself is the basic human need, but the way an individual communicates emanates from his or her culture. In other words, communication is a product of culture. This can be seen in the fact that when communicating, some cultures prefer debate, while others value silence more. Therefore, "communication is culture, and culture is communication" (Hall, 1976).

1.4 Review Tasks

Ⅰ. Decide whether the following statements are true (T) or false (F).

1. Culture is a static entity while communication is a dynamic process.　　　　( )

2. Culture can be seen as shared knowledge, what people need to know in order to act appropriately in a given culture.　　　　( )

3. Generally speaking, culture refers to a shared background resulting from a common

Chapter One
Culture and Communication

language and communication style, customs, beliefs, attitudes and values. ( )

4. Cultural mistakes are more serious than linguistic mistakes. Linguistic mistakes mean that someone is not fully expressing his or her idea while cultural mistakes can lead to serious misunderstanding and even ill-feeling between individuals. ( )

5. All people of the same nationality will have the same culture. ( )

6. Culture enables us to communicate with others through a language that we have learned and that we share in common. ( )

7. Although two cultures may share the same ideas, their meaning and significance may not be the same. ( )

8. One's actions are totally independent of his or her culture. ( )

9. A culture is but one link in the whole chain of generations, some of which have become history and some of which are in transition. ( )

10. Everyone has a unique style of communication but cultures determine a general style for their members. ( )

11. Verbal communication refers to methods of conversation which only include spoken words. ( )

12. Communication and culture are separable and weakly connected. ( )

13. Communication is a dynamic, systematic process in which meanings are created and reflected in human interaction with symbols. ( )

14. The way that an archaeologist is deciphering a mysterious sign on the recently unearthed pot cannot be regarded as a form of communication. ( )

15. Once a communication event takes place, it is irreversible. ( )

16. Communication itself is the basic human need, so the way an individual communicates doesn't emanate from his or her culture. ( )

17. Humans are symbol-making creatures so human symbolic communication is man's alone. ( )

18. Communication permeates our life, and our life is guided by our cultures. ( )

19. Communication permits us to express our thoughts and feelings to others, but cannot satisfy our emotional and material needs. ( )

20. Verbal communication includes speaking, hearing, writing and reading. ( )

II. **Discuss the following questions.**

1. What is communication? What role does it play in your life?
2. What is culture? How important is it to you?
3. What do you think is the relationship between culture and communication?

III. **Analyze the following cases and answer the questions.**

Case one

An American woman received a letter from a recently married Japanese friend. The Japanese woman wrote in her letter, "My husband is not very handsome. Your husband is much more handsome than mine." The American woman was very surprised at what her friend wrote.

Questions

1. Why was the American surprised?
2. Why did the Japanese woman write, "My husband is not very handsome"?

Case two

Xin Yu had been studying at a large well-known university overseas for seven years. He had settled into a sound routine of hard work and spent almost all of his time revising, researching and improving his English writing.

In particular, he had a special effort with his first term essay. He had carefully researched the topic, finding several excellent books in the library. His first draft had been completed with great difficulty but he had preserved and re-written the essay, ensuring that the material was relevant and that the language was the best he could write. He was pleased that he had handed in before time.

Upon receiving the essay back from lecturer, he was very disappointed not only with the C+ mark but with the marker's comments, "This is a satisfactory first attempt but it lacks originality. In fact it borders on repetition of the actual authors' work—in that sense it is close to plagiarism. Please see me as soon as possible."

Xin Yu was horrified and worried. So much effort, so many books and now he was summoned to meet the lecturer. He could not understand what the problem was.

Questions

1. What advice do you think the lecturer would give to Xin Yu?
2. What points do you think Xin Yu would give to his lecturer in regard to his essay?

IV. Extended Reading.

Passage one

How to Improve Communication Skills

Communication that crosses cultural boundaries can be fraught with misunderstanding. Gestures and language that mean one thing to you can mean something entirely different to a person from another tribe or tongue. A globalized economy has brought greater diversity to communities that were once singular in their ethnic composition. Ignorance of history and experience can lead to comments that ignite old wounds, or worse, offend outright. Fortunately, you can take steps to help put your best foot forward toward mutual understanding and respect.

Study the history of the other cultures

Understanding past challenges and injustices ethnic groups have suffered at the hands of others goes a long way toward cultivating social sensitivity. Learning cultural history provides alternate perspectives to past events.

Learn the nonverbal language used by other cultures

Conflict resolution expert Michelle LeBaron says, "Nonverbal communication is hugely important in any interaction with others; its importance is multiplied across cultures. This is because we tend to look for nonverbal cues when verbal messages are unclear or ambiguous." Simply put, if there's already a language barrier, make sure gestures and facial expressions are understood to be respectful and conciliatory.

Understand different attitudes towards "saving face"

Some cultures place the utmost importance on personal honor. Others view honor in terms of the group they represent. Less formal cultures can overlook the importance of language or comments that can be perceived as dishonoring to another culture. Become familiar with traditions or etiquette practiced by other cultures. Use language understood to esteem the individual or their group.

Recognize different perceptions of time

Western cultures view time as a commodity that must be tightly managed. Eastern and indigenous cultures tend to view time as more elastic and relative. Ignorance of this dynamic can lead to the perception of communication being rushed and the individual being less important than the event.

Avoid rushes to judgment

According to noted anthropologists Kevin Avruch and Peter Black, "... when faced by an interaction that we do not understand, people tend to interpret the others involved as 'abnormal', 'weird', or 'wrong'". People can detect when they are being judged as unusual or out of the norm. This unwitting condescension can lead to a breakdown in meaningful communication. When others are treated as though their ideas have intrinsic value, they are more receptive to seeing the value in the ideas of others.

Continually practice

Effective cross-cultural communication requires time and patience. Mistakes are inevitable as you learn the needs and sensitivities of those who may have a different world view. Persistent engagement will help you form the skills needed to develop effective cross-cultural communication.

(*Adapted from http://www.ehow.com/how_2080970.html*)

Questions

1. What are the effective steps to research the mutual understanding and respect in intercultural communication, according to the passage?

2. How could you understand the sentence "Nonverbal communication is hugely important in any interaction with others; its importance is multiplied across cultures." in the passage?

Passage two

How Verbal & Nonverbal Communication Can Sometimes Be Misinterpreted

The misinterpretation of communication can have dire consequences. People who misinterpret communication burn bridges, offend superiors and make enemies, all while having the most positive of intentions. Adding to this problem is the fact that communication is complex; people can often give seemingly contradictory verbal and nonverbal signals that obscure their intended meaning. There are many ways that verbal and nonverbal communication can be misinterpreted, most having to do with ambiguity, cultural differences and mixed messages.

Ambiguity

Ambiguous words are one of the main sources of misinterpretation in verbal communication. Words that have more than one meaning cause misinterpretations if used in the wrong context. For example, when said out loud, the phrase "he makes a lot" could mean that a person creates a lot of things and makes money from it, or creates things while earning no money, or earns a lot of money from passive investments. The three possible interpretations stem from the fact that "make" can mean to produce something (as in a product) or to obtain something (as in money or a goal). Verbal misinterpretations such as these can be compounded by vague and imprecise language.

Cultural Differences

Cultural differences can contribute to misinterpretation in verbal and nonverbal communication. In verbal communication, cultural differences can contribute to the misinterpretation of words. For example, the word "Jihad" is often translated into English as "holy war", but in Arabic it is more similar in meaning to "struggle", whether militarily or spiritually. In nonverbal communication, differences in the meaning of gestures can contribute to misinterpretation as well. For example, putting your head down in Western cultures is a sign of low self-confidence, whereas in Japanese culture it is a sign of respect.

Mixed Messages

Sometimes, the meaning of a word appears clear but is belied by body language that sends another message. For example, when a person says "I'd like to meet you again" while crossing his arms and avoiding eye contact, it could be difficult for that person's interlocutor to determine whether he is being sincere. Other times, nonverbal signals appear to contradict each other; for example, crossed arms (suggesting defensiveness) and a warm smile (suggesting openness).

Social Awkwardness

Sometimes, people are simply awkward in getting their messages across. When people speak monotonously and without tone or body language, it can be difficult to ascertain any message from their communication at all. When people are experiencing severe social anxiety, they sometimes speak too quietly to be heard. People with Asperger's syndrome often have trouble sending their intended message with verbal and nonverbal communication because of its notorious difficulty to read.

Conflict

When people are on guard in a social situation, they could be overly vigilant and on the lookout for insults and slights. For example, if a person has been told that another person does not think highly of him, that person might read too much into neutral body language and come to conclusions about hidden meanings behind neutral communications. Two people on opposite sides of a conflict (for example, mutual friends of either party in a lawsuit) could interpret hostile signs from one another when none was intended, due to both being on guard and on the lookout for negative messages.

(Adapted from http://www.ehow.com/how_2080970.html)

Questions

1. What may cause the misinterpretation of verbal and nonverbal communication according to the passage?

2. Can you give an example of the misinterpretation of verbal or nonverbal communication?

Intercultural Communication

> *Diversity will be the engine that drives the corporation of the 21st Century.*
>
> —Stephen H. Rhinesmith
>
> *Studying a second language without learning the culture is like learning how to drive a car by studying a driver's manual and never getting behind a steering wheel.*
>
> —K. J. Irving

2.1　Lead-in Cases

Case one

Early during the Suzuki family's stay in the United States, Mr. Suzuki went out after work with several American businessmen. They went to a small restaurant and ordered a pitcher of beer. As is the custom in Japan, Mr. Suzuki filled the glass of everyone at the table but himself. He left his own glass empty. The American men at the table looked at Mr. Suzuki in surprise. One asked if Mr. Suzuki didn't want a drink. Mr. Suzuki smiled and nodded. The men waited for him to fill his own glass. When he did not, they dismissed it and began to talk. Throughout the night, the Americans continued to fill their own glasses or had them filled by Mr. Suzuki. They assumed that Mr. Suzuki did not drink and left his glass empty.

Intercultural Communication — Chapter Two

Questions

1. Why did Mr. Suzuki leave his own glass empty?
2. What would a Chinese man do in similar situations?

Case two

Kenneth, an American student, met Vernon, a student who recently arrived from Malaysia, and they decided to have dinner together at the university cafeteria. In the cafeteria, Kenneth ordered a pizza and some other food for their dinner. When the food was sent to them, Kenneth tore the pizza into pieces and handed one piece to Vernon, using his left hand. Vernon took that piece of pizza and put it on his plate without eating it. Kenneth was quite confused about what had gone wrong, so he asked Vernon, "Are you all right?" "Yes, I'm fine," Vernon replied. Kenneth kept on asking, "Why don't you eat the pizza?" Vernon said nothing but began to eat the other food, ignoring the pizza. Kenneth was confused but he ceased his questioning. And the two just kept on eating without much conversation.

Questions

1. Why didn't Vernon eat the pizza?
2. How would you help to explain Vernon's behavior?
3. Which form of intercultural communication does their communication belong to?

2.2 What Is Intercultural Communication?

Intercultural communication occurs whenever there is communication between people from different cultural backgrounds, for example, what happened on the Silk Road, Marco Polo's stay in China, Monk Jianzhen's mission to Japan, and Zhen He's seven voyages to the Western Seas—they tell us that intercultural communication is as old as history. Nevertheless, as a discipline, its history is short.

Intercultural communication as a field of study first emerged in the U. S. in the 1950s as a result of the four trends that lead to the development of the global village:

• Convenient transportation system: In the form of transportation and communication systems, new technology has accelerated intercultural contact. Supersonic transports now

17

make it possible for tourists, business executives, or government officials to enjoy breakfast in San Francisco and dinner in Paris.

- Innovative communication systems: Innovative communication systems have also encouraged and facilitated cultural interaction. Communication satellites, sophisticated television transmission equipment, and digital switching networks now allow people throughout the world to share information and ideas instantaneously.
- Economic globalization: As we enter the 21st century, the United States is no longer the dominant economic force in the world. For example, according to Harris and Moran (Samovar & Porter, 2003), there are now more than 37,000 transnational corporations with 207,000 foreign affiliates. This expansion in globalization has resulted in multinational corporations participating in joint ventures, licensing agreements and other international business arrangements.
- Widespread migrations: In the United States, people are now redefining and rethinking the meaning of the word "American". It can no longer be used to describe a somewhat homogeneous group of people sharing a European heritage. As Ben J. Wattenberg tells us, America has become the first universal nation, a truly multi-cultural society marked by unparalleled diversity. (Samovar & Porter, 2003)

Edward Hall is considered the father of intercultural communication with his publication of *The Silent Language* in 1959 and his many other works. The 1960s was the period of conceptualization of the field by communication scholars. The 1970s showed a rapid development, reflected in the publication of numerous studies. During the 1980s, the field moved toward integration and a clear identity. The 1990s stressed diversification of methods, displayed increased concern with domestic co-cultures, and also witnessed efforts to redress historical and colonial imbalances. By the end of the 20th century, there were as many as nineteen specific intercultural communication theories put forward. (Gudykunst, 2003)

What is intercultural communication? Generally speaking, intercultural communication refers to communication between people whose cultural backgrounds are distinct enough to alter their communication. Cultural influence on individuals and the problems inherent in the production and interpretation of messages in intercultural communications are illustrated in the Figure 2.1 by Samovar & Porter.

Here, three cultures are represented by three distinct geometric shapes. Cultures A and B are similar to one another and are purposely represented by a square and an irregular octagon that resembles a square. Culture C is intended to be quite different from Cultures A and B and is differentiated both by its circular shape and its physical distance from Cultures A and B. Within each represented culture is another form similar to the shape of the influencing parent culture. This form represents a person who has been molded by his or her culture. The shape representing the person, however, is somewhat different from that of the parent culture due to various individualistic factors such as gender, age, class, status, etc.

Chapter Two
Intercultural Communication

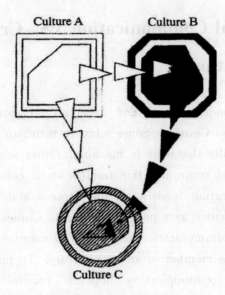

Figure 2.1

The amount of influence a culture has in intercultural communication varies depending on its similarity with another culture, which is marked by both shape and distance in the figure. The more similarities two cultures share, the less influence culture will have on communication. Therefore, the fewer messages will be changed during communication; the less the cultures are alike, the greater the influence of culture on communication will be, and the more likely the messages will be changed. Misunderstanding in intercultural communication often arises here. In this figure, the variation in shape and distance indicates that Culture A is more similar to Culture B than it is to Culture C. If we take Chinese culture as Culture A and Japanese culture as Culture B, we can suppose Culture C to be American culture. If people from Chinese culture go to Japan, due to the similarities between Chinese and Japanese cultures, they can communicate with Japanese people without causing much misunderstanding. Or, people of the Japanese culture could understand most of what they say without their messages being altered too much. However, when Chinese people communicate with American people, problems often occur because Chinese culture and American Culture differ from each other greatly.

Questions

1. What are the contributions of Edward Hall to the study of intercultural communication?

2. Discuss the four trends that make our world more interdependent.

3. Discuss the relationship between the technological development and the intercultural communication.

2.3 Intercultural Communication VS. Cross-cultural Communication

Both cross-cultural communication and intercultural communication have been translated as "跨文化交际" in Chinese. Some scholars maintain that these two terms are interchangeable, being basically the same in meaning. Other scholars argue that they are different in that cross-cultural communication implies static comparison between cultures while intercultural communication focuses on the process and interaction. Intercultural communication may be understood as a practice, called in Chinese "跨文化交际". As the term suggests, intercultural communication occurs when a member of one culture produces a message for consumption by a member of another culture. To put it simply, intercultural communication means the communication between people from different cultural backgrounds. It consists of several levels of communication.

2.4 Case Discussion

Case one

Angela, a Canadian, married a Chinese engineer Joe Wang in the States. Later Joe's mother came to visit them from Hangzhou, China. The next day after her arrival, Angela talked to Joe while his mother was playing with their little son Jeremy in the garden.

Angela: Joe, how long is your mum going to stay?
Joe: I don't know. I haven't asked her.
Angela: Why not ask her?
Joe: How could I ask her?
Angela: Why not? I just want to ask her how long she's going to stay.

To Angela's great puzzlement, the next day, her mother-in-law told them that she would leave for Hangzhou in a week. It seemed that the mother had overheard their conversation. But why?

Questions

1. What went wrong with Angela and her mother-in-law?
2. What would you do if you were in the case?

Case two

Sue, an English teacher, had a birthday party at home last weekend. It was a good time, but she was a bit upset by one of her guests, Yang, a Chinese girl who has just come to the States. The following is their initial conversation:

Sue: Oh, Yang, how nice you could come!
Yang: Hi, Sue. Happy birthday!
Sue: Thanks! Come on in. Can I take your coat?
Yang: No, thanks.
Sue: Ok, this way please.
Yang: (takes off her coat and hangs it.)
Sue: ...? (feels upset and a little bit strange)

Questions

1. Why was Sue upset?
2. What would be appropriate for Yang to do and to say in this situation?

Case three

Professor Wang had written a book on Chinese but knew a little English. Last year he got to know an American Professor Johnson who was to learn Chinese culture in a seminar. One day before Professor Johnson went back to America, Professor Wang decided to give him his book as a gift.

Prof. Wang: Mr. Johnson, this is a clumsy book written by your humble servant.
Prof. Johnson: Who is my humble servant? You? No, no, no, you're not my humble servant. You are kidding, Prof. Wang.
Prof. Wang: No, I am not kidding. It's true. And I would like to give it to you as a gift. I am sorry for this small gift.
Prof. Johnson: Oh, great. Thank you. I like it very much. What's it about?

Questions

1. What are the communication problems?
2. How would you explain the reasons for their misunderstandings?

2.5 Group Discussion

Situation 1: A Washington state agriculture official who was touring China a few years ago handed out bright green baseball caps at every stop without noticing that none of the men would put them on or that all women were giggling.

Situation 2: A leading U.S golf ball manufacturer targeted Japan as an important new market for its product, but even after heavy advertising, the sales of the company's golf products were well below average. As it turned out, the firm had offered its product in white packaging, and in groups of four.

Situation 3: A Chinese student had just arrived in the States. One day, when reading in his room, he heard someone shouting outside: "Watch out!" So he went to the window and stretched out his head and tried to find out what's going on outside. Just then, his head was right poured by the water from above...

2.6 Further Reading

Improving Intercultural Communication

Know yourself

What you bring to the communication event greatly influences the success or failure of that event. Although the idea of knowing yourself is common, it is nevertheless crucial to improving intercultural communication. The novelist James Baldwin said it best when he wrote, "The questions which one asks oneself begin, at least to illuminate the world, and become one's key to the experience of others." Baldwin's remarks serve as an ideal introduction for the portion of this book that urges you to begin your path to improvement with some self-analysis. As with many of the suggestions we offer in this section, it is easier to state the advice than to practice it. We can write the words "know yourself" with just a few strokes on our keyboard, but it will take a great deal of effort for you to translate this assignment into practice. We believe that the application of introspection should take three directions: first, know your culture; second, know your perceptions; and third, know how you act on those perceptions. Although these three concepts work in tandem, it might be useful to examine them separately.

Know your culture

Your first step toward introspection should begin with your own culture, regardless of what that culture might be. Remember, we are products of our culture—and culture helps control communication. Steward and Bennett made a similar observation when they wrote "An awareness of American culture along with the example of contrasting culture contributes to the individual's understanding of oneself as a cultural being".

Know your attitudes

By exhorting you to examine your attitudes and perceptions, we are not referring to any mystical notions involving another reality, nor are we suggesting you engage in a deep psychological soul searching. Rather, we are asking you to identify those attitudes, prejudices, and opinions that we all carry around and that bias the way the word appears to us. If we hold a certain attitude toward gay men, and a man who is a gay talks to us, our pre-communication attitude will color our response to what he says. Knowing our likes, dislikes, and degrees of personal ethnocentrism enables us to place them out in the open so that we can detect the ways in which these attitudes influence communication.

Know your communication style

The third step in knowing ourselves is somewhat more difficult than simply identifying our prejudices and predispositions. It involves discovering the kind of image we portray to the rest of the world. Ask yourself, "How do I communicate and how do others perceive me?" If you perceive yourself in one way, and the people with whom you interact perceive you in another way, serious problem can arise. We have all heard stories of how foreigners view Americans traveling abroad. The "Ugly American" example might be old and trite, but our experiences continue to reinforce its truth. If we are to improve our communication, we must, therefore, have some idea of how we present ourselves. If, for instance, you see yourself as patient and calm, but you appear rushed and anxious, you will have a hard time understanding why people respond to you as they do. As we have noted elsewhere, our most taken-for-granted behaviors are often hidden from consciousness.

(*Larry A. Samovar, Richard E. Porter, Lisa A. Stefani*, 2004:251)

Questions

1. According to the passage, what are the steps of improving intercultural communication? Explain them in your own words.

2. Which step is the hardest one in your opinion?

2.7 Review Tasks

Ⅰ. **Decide whether the following statements are true (T) or false (F).**

(1) Intercultural Communication as a discipline first started in Europe.　　(　)

(2) In intercultural communication, we should separate one's individual character from cultural generalization.　　(　)

(3) An awareness of one's own culture can help one to improve his/her intercultural

communication. ( )

(4) Culture can be learned through proverbs, folktales, legends, myths, mass media, and so on. ( )

(5) Learning to understand people whose background is different from your own is an easy assignment. ( )

(6) Innovative communication systems have also encouraged and facilitated cultural interaction. ( )

(7) Culture is like an iceberg, and only some of the culture is visible. ( )

(8) Culture strongly influences your beliefs, values, and world views. But it can't shape your relationships with your family and friends. ( )

(9) Intercultural communication refers to communication between people whose cultural backgrounds are distinct enough to alter their communication. ( )

(10) Our own native language and culture are so much a part of us that we take them for granted. ( )

(11) The more similarities two cultures share, the more messages will be changed during communication. ( )

(12) The less similarities two cultures share, the more likely the messages will be changed. ( )

(13) In fact, most researchers agree that culture refers to beliefs, norms, and attitudes that are used to guide our behaviors and to solve human problems. ( )

(14) Intercultural communication is as old as history and as a discipline it has a very long history. ( )

(15) Concepts of dress, time, language, manners and nonverbal behavior can differ significantly among cultures. ( )

(16) Edward Hall is considered the father of intercultural communication with his publication of the Silent Language in 1959. ( )

(17) Some scholars maintain that two terms of cross-cultural communication and intercultural communication are interchangeable, being basically the same in meaning. ( )

(18) One's own attitude in communication will not influence his/her intercultural communication too much. ( )

(19) Since we are products of our culture, knowing ourselves is crucial to improving intercultural communication. ( )

(20) If we are to improve our communication, we must, therefore, have some idea of how we present ourselves. ( )

II. Discuss the following questions.

1. What does intercultural communication mean to you?

2. What accounts for the difficulties in conducting communication across cultures?

3. What do you think usually leads to misunderstanding in intercultural communication?

Chapter Two — Intercultural Communication

Ⅲ. **Analyze the following cases and answer the questions.**

Case one — Overdone Chinese Hospitality

Joe is an Assistant Professor in an American university. Two years ago, he made friends with Hong, a Chinese visiting scholar in another American university when he was in the final year of his PhD program. He began teaching in a university after graduation. Hong who had been back to China recommended Joe to her university. Soon, Joe was invited by Hong's university for a five-day visit.

Joe was very excited about the trip, as it was his first time to China. Hong and the Chair of her Department met him at the airport, and then put him up in a nice hotel. They had arranged a big dinner for him for the evening and made Joe feel very welcome. At the end of the evening, Hong gave him the itinerary for the next few days. Apart from the lectures, all his time would be filled with meals, concerts, shopping, and a one-day trip to a nearby resort, all paid by the university. Joe had thought he would have time to explore the city and the area, but the itinerary would leave him no free time.

Joe was grateful to Hong and the Chair of the Department who took great care of him during his visit. At the end of the visit, he insisted on treating Hong and the Chair of the Department to dinner to thank them. But they said a dinner had been arranged. Joe was very frustrated. He was not very happy at the dinner, and did not show any enthusiasm when the Chair of the Department said that they hoped Joe would come back for another visit.

When it came time for Joe to leave, he did not know what to say. He knew he should be grateful to everything Hong had done for him, but he had also felt deprived and trapped since he never found the time to do anything by himself. The tight itinerary never allowed him to explore on his own; he felt especially annoyed that all the plans had been made without consulting him. As soon as Joe left, Hong was very relieved. She felt Joe's visit had been successful. She never knew that Joe, still upset about the tight control placed on his schedule, complained to the person sitting next to him on the plane, "During the visit, I sometimes felt like a prisoner!"

Questions

1. How do you comment on the behaviors of Hong and Joe respectively?
2. If you were Joe, how would you respond to such situation?
3. What suggestions would you like to give Hong on hosting a friend from another

culture?

Case two   Ambiguous Time

Fan learned to drive when she was studying in the United States. On the day she bought her car, she parked it on the street closest to her apartment. She was excited about being able to drive her own car to school the next day and did not notice a small piece of paper under the windshield wiper blade on the front window of the car until she stopped for a red light. Her heart sank. It looked like a ticket.

She jumped out of the car at the first chance. It was indeed a ticket—a ticket for illegal parking. She would have to pay a $30 fine. She was confused about the reason for the ticket until it dawned on her that she had misinterpreted the warning sign for parking on the street. She did know that parking was not allowed on that street from 12:00 a.m. which meant 12:00 noon for her Chinese mind, while in the States, it meant 12:00 midnight. She parked on the street that evening because she thought she would leave for school well before noon the next day!

Before paying the fine, Fan explained to the official about the Chinese interpretation of time, stating that she would not have parked there if she had known 12:00 a.m. in America meant 12:00 p.m. for the Chinese. The official thought for a while and said, "Since there's a cultural difference here, I'm going to ask you to pay $15 instead of $30."

Questions

1. Why did Fan make such a mistake?
2. Why did the official decide to make a less severe punishment?
3. What can we learn from the case above?

IV. Extended Reading.

Passage one

The Advantages of Intercultural Communication

Global interconnectivity has made intercultural communication critical for any organization. Intercultural communication takes place with people of different cultures discussing and communicating. Businesses intending to operate globally should invest in intercultural training for their staff to enjoy the immense benefits. Effective intercultural communication produces benefits such as employee productivity and teamwork.

Productivity and Proficiency

Intercultural communication helps employees from different ethnic backgrounds to communicate effectively with one another. It also guides the management competencies to design policies that incorporate the diversity in the team, allowing every member to be productive and proficient in their tasks. Since employees are well trained in intercultural communication, it eliminates misunderstanding and dissatisfaction that may arise if employees' needs are not put into consideration while developing policies, planning for meetings, and designing incentive schemes. Satisfied employees are able to focus on their duties, thereby increasing productivity.

Teamwork

Intercultural communication fosters teamwork in an organization. It helps staff to understand each other's cultural differences, and to communicate effectively without misunderstanding. With successful intercultural communication, employees understand the influence of culture on peoples' behavior and communication tendencies. This enhances teamwork, as colleagues respect one another's cultural background, unique talents and capabilities, which is key to the smooth running of business. Since employees are aware of their colleagues' cultural influences, intercultural communication eliminates stereotyping—a danger to effective communication and team work.

Global Business Edge

Successful intercultural communication gives an organization a global business edge. Training employees in intercultural communication gives an organization of successful negotiation skills in the global market of diverse cultures. A company venturing its business in Africa will have a receptive welcome if it understands important cultural factors crucial to business transactions. Some cultural traits important to transacting business in Africa are time, religion, handshakes, communication tactics and respect towards seniors. A company that understands the importance of cross-cultural communication has advantages in launching its business globally over a company that has not invested in it.

Effective Leadership

Intercultural communication also fosters effective leadership in an organization. Modern organizations are composed of diverse people, and managers are expected to lead their teams by creating understanding of the company's policies while accommodating the diverse views of his team. A company that equips its leadership team in intercultural training enables them to motivate their teams, regardless of their cultural background. Intercultural training builds effective communication, which is a step toward effective leadership.

(*Adapted from http://www.intercultural.org/siic.php*)

Questions

1. What are the benefits of intercultural communication in running business?

2. Why does the successful intercultural communication improve the teamwork's efficiency?

Passage two

Six Barriers to Intercultural Communication

Even within the same culture, communication isn't always easy. Spouses get divorced, friends fall out and workers change jobs—often because of misunderstandings. Add cultural differences to the mix, and the sources of potential problems multiply. Whether you're a student, businessperson or traveler, knowing the barriers to intercultural communication is the first step to overcoming problems.

Language Differences

Language differences are an obvious barrier to intercultural communication. If you speak only English and a shopkeeper speaks only Japanese, you won't be able to communicate verbally. Even if you've studied the language or an interpreter is available, dialects, different accents and slang can cause problems. In addition, words don't necessarily translate from one language to another in a clean one-to-one correspondence. The same English word may have different meanings to people from different cultures.

Body Language

People sometimes take offense because of differences in body language across cultures. For example, a businessperson from Latin America might stand closer to a client than someone from North America would. This may make the North American feel crowded and want to back away. People from southern Europe typically use more eye contact than Britons and Americans, which may make the English-speakers uncomfortable. Because the French typically smile less than Americans, sometimes Americans think they aren't friendly.

Level of Context

Most English-speaking cultures are low-context, meaning they put a message into explicit words. In these cultures, saying "no" when you mean "no" is just considered straight forward or honest. High-context cultures, such as Japan, expect the listener to pick up more meaning from the general situation. For example, Asians sometimes say "yes" or "maybe" when they actually mean "no", according to the Diversity Council. Asians often consider an outright refusal blunt rather than honest.

Value of Time

Not all cultures think about time in the North American linear fashion. In the U.S., punctuality is important, but Latin and Middle Eastern cultures put a higher value on relationships. For example, you'd finish your conversation with someone even if it makes you late to a meeting. A culture's view of time also influences how it sees deadlines. For example, North Americans consider making a deadline crucial—whether on the job or in college. People from Asia or South America are more likely to view deadlines as less important than results over the long haul.

Negative Stereotypes and Prejudices

Stereotypes and prejudices about people from other cultures can cause communication problems and give offense. Ethnocentrism, or a belief that your own culture is better than that of others, can lead to acting superior toward other groups and not treating them well. For example, a teacher in an American college may think that students from a certain culture lack strong English skills or are incapable of good work. This prejudice can lead the teacher to treat the students unfairly.

Feelings and Emotions

Individuals from the United Kingdom and Japan typically keep a tight control of their emotions, while Italians and French are more comfortable showing their feelings. Loud talking might embarrass an Englishman, for example, but an Italian may just be expressing excitement. Differences in culture and communication styles can even cause fear. As a result of this anxiety, people from different cultures may pull back and avoid trying to communicate at all, reports Kathy McKeiver, Coordinator of International Student Academic Advising at Northern Arizona University and Chair of the Global Engagement Commission of the National Academic Advising Association.

(Adapted from http://www.intercultural.org/siic.php)

Questions

1. What are the barriers in intercultural communication according to the passage?
2. Which of them do you think is not easy to overcome?

Daily Verbal Intercultural Communication

When in Rome, do as the Romans do.

—*English Proverb*

Every tale can be told in a different way.

—*Greek Proverb*

3.1 Lead-in Cases

Case one

When I first went to Hong Kong, I had no idea about Chinese tea-drinking and found myself caught in a very awkward situation. I visited a Chinese family and was immediately given a cup of tea. I was not thirsty and I did not particularly like that type of tea, but out of politeness I finished the cup. But the more I drank, the more I was given. I kept insisting that I did not want any more, but the host took no notice. I drank about twelve cups of tea that afternoon! The host must have thought I was very greedy, but I did not know how to avoid getting more tea poured.

Question

How could you help "I" in this case out of the awkward situation?

Case two

Lisa was taken aback by her host putting food onto her plate because this seldom happens in her country. Lisa kept finishing all the food on her plate because she wished to be polite. That was a big mistake because she found her plate refilled and many more dishes following.

Question

How to analyze Lisa's problem?

3.2 Hospitality

Hospitality, which refers to the friendly and generous reception and entertainment of guests, visitors, or strangers, is universal, but what is hospitality varies from culture to culture. Trouble may result if you are ignorant of the conventional practices of hospitality in cultures other than your own.

3.2.1 Different Aspects of Hospitality

• British hospitality on eating: In Britain, hospitality is not measured by how many dishes are provided as in China. It is shown by giving you freedom to choose whatever you really want. People never press you. They hardly put food on your plate but just ask you to help yourself. So if you, as a guest, are shy or modest, waiting for the food to be put on your plate, you will be disappointed.

• Chinese hospitality on eating: In China, people's hospitality is shown by the number of the dishes offered, as well as by the eagerness to impress the guest with the most expensive and nutritious food.

• Where to eat? As an English saying goes, "An Englishman's home is his castle", westerners usually invite their friends to eat at home, except in some important occasions such as Christmas or Thanksgiving, to express their hospitality. In Chinese culture, however, inviting friends out in the restaurant for dinner could always give the guests a good impression that they are greatly valued.

• What to eat? In China, an informal dinner would have four dishes and a soup; a formal dinner would have at least eight dishes and a soup. Chinese usually show their hospitality through the quantity of the dishes. In Britain, people value equality. Their hospitality is shown by treating the guest as an equal with the host. Believing in simplicity and frugality regarding food, they may offer their guest the same type of meal they usually eat. Part of the reason is their egalitarianism, and another reason is that the host wants to introduce British food and eating customs to the foreign guest. Even if it was a formal dinner, there would be usually just three courses: appetizer, main dish and dessert. Besides, westerners emphasize more on the atmosphere and interaction at the table rather than eating itself. Moreover, westerners seldom consider organs of animals or some special parts like fish head and chicken feet as edible food, while in Chinese culture, they are popular dishes at dinner table.

- How much to eat? If a Westerner is invited to have dinner at a Chinese family, he/she would probably feel awkward by the scene that Chinese host/hostess constantly fill his/her plate with more food, or ask the guest to eat more even when the guest already feels full. Chinese show hospitality and warmth by offering the guests enough food to eat, expecting that the prepared dishes at the table are "more" than what guests could eat. Contrarily, Western hosts/hostesses would expect their prepared dishes to be exactly what everyone needs, and in their eyes, waste of food is intolerable.

- Chinese hospitality on treating people: Most Chinese people are hospitable to their guests, friends and relatives who are called "in-group members" but tend to be indifferent to the strangers who are labeled "out-group members".

- Western hospitality on treating people: On the contrary, in the eyes of Westerners', strangers are not always treated with indifference. Believing in equality and showing respect for individual rights, they are hospitable to their guests, friends and relatives, but may also be hospitable to strangers. There can also be situations when a westerner seems to be very polite and nice to the strangers but not polite to friends or relatives.

3.2.2 Case Discussion

Case one

The first six or seven dishes seemed to fill the table to overflowing, with plates precariously wedged one on top of another. With my American-bred expectations, I assumed this vast first wave of food was surely the total number of dishes to be served, and I dug in greedily, dazzled by the variety and sheer quantity. The Chinese guests around me, however, had a different reaction. They seemed merely to take a bite or two of each dish and then put their chopsticks down, continuing to chat. "They must not be very hungry," I thought with a shrug, and continued my feast.

To my surprise, more dishes soon were piled on top of the already mountainous stack. Plus two or three soups, side dishes, desserts, and delicacies of various kinds, all seemingly enough to feed the entire People's Liberation Army. No wonder my fellow guests had merely sampled a few bites of each dish; they knew very well that these first few items were just the tip of a titanic culinary iceberg. I, however, was so stuffed after the first fifteen minutes that I could only watch in a bloated stupor as the remainder of the banquet took its course.

Question

Can you see some characteristics of the Chinese way of entertaining guests to dinner from the above?

Case two

Peter was one of the American technicians who came to China to help set up a coffee plant. He was in China for six months. Before leaving for home, one of his Chinese colleagues took him out to dinner. Peter decided to ask him a question that had puzzled him for as long as he worked in the plant.

"Why is it that the Chinese workers are given stainless boxes for their lunch, while we foreigners have lunch put in the disposable plastic boxes?"

The colleague smiled, "It is because the plastic boxes are more convenient—they are disposable. With the stainless boxes, you have to wash them after every meal."

But Peter was not convinced. "I don't think so. Stainless boxes are much better than plastic boxes. They look more professional, they are more durable, and they protect your lunch better."

Questions

1. How was the well-intentioned practice on the Chinese side ill-interpreted in the above case?
2. Try to offer at least two possible reasons for each side.

3.3 Greeting

Greetings are common ways of human interactions in both English and Chinese cultures. When people meet, they usually greet each other. The purpose of the greeting is to establish or maintain social contact, not to transfer information, so formulaic expressions are often used, such as "have you had lunch?", which would be regarded as an indirect invitation to lunch, and between unmarried young people it indicates a young man's interest in dating a girl in British culture. In Chinese culture, it has no real signification at all, it is merely a greeting.

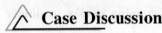

Case

You represent Guangzhou Industrial Product Import and Export Corporation, and you are assigned to meet an American business person——Ronald Vannburg, Marketing Manager of the wholesaler, Vallery View Company—at the airport. You and Vannburg have never met each other before, so you say greetings, ask him how his flight was and show him to the car.

Question

Please act this out with another student in the class.

3.4 Concern

When someone is sick, e.g. having a cold, in China, it is common to hear the following expressions:

Drink plenty of water.

Put on more clothes.

These pieces of advice are in fact just expressions of concern. Westerners often feel their privacy offended at being told such things. Such phrases have protective, parental overtones, and hence may sound inappropriate to the independent westerners.

The concern is normally shown in English by phrases such as:

I do hope you'll be feeling better soon.

Look after yourself.

Have you been to the doctor?

Try and get some rest.

Case Discussion

Case one

"Don't try to teach your grandmother how to suck eggs." is an English proverb, implying that one should never show wrong concern with a good intention. Due to the cultural differences, Chinese have their particular way of showing concern to their friends or strangers, which from Westerners' perspective is an insult of their self-dignity, sometimes with an inclination of compelling. In the following situations, we may understand how inappropriate Chinese show their concern to Westerners.

— When a Westerner catches a cold, a Chinese says, "You should drink more water."

— When a Westerner is ready to go outside for a picnic, a Chinese says, "You should put on more clothes."

— When a 60-year-old Western tourist comes to travel, a Chinese tour guide says, "You must be tired. You're old..."

What are the appropriate ways of showing concern in the above situations?

— "I hope you'll be feeling better soon."/ "Take good care of yourself."

— "Enjoy yourself."/ "Have a good time."

"How are you doing now? A little rest wouldn't do us any harm, would it?"

Case two

In China, when seeing someone carrying something relatively big or heavy, people would usually go to offer a help. Out of politeness, this person will refuse by saying, "It's no big deal. Thank you." But the helper will continue for the second or even the third time to offer help. This "offer-refusal" would go on repeating back and forth until finally the receiver gives up.

This "goodness" of Chinese people, however, is not considered as a virtue. Once, a

Chinese student, studying in Britain, underwent the exact "offer-refusal" process to help his teacher to bring some studying materials to her office. Finally, his teacher said, "Thank you. In fact, it's not very heavy."

Case three

A Chinese is studying in the US. One day, he found a new roommate moving in his apartment and was moving a mattress into the house. He went up to the American roommate and said "Shall I help you?" To his little upset, the young man said, "You need not do it. But if you really want to, you can do it."

3.5 Money

Money is an important concern of conversation in daily verbal communications. When people talk about money issues, for example, when borrowing or lending money, they may show a sharp contrast in their attitudes and behaviors in different cultures. Chinese and Westerners also hold different concepts towards saving and spending. Besides, people also talk in different ways concerning the price in purchasing.

3.5.1 Case Discussion

Case one

While I was studying in America, I met an American named Jimmy. One day I was eager to buy a book, but I did not have enough money, so I borrowed three dollars from him. Before he lent me the three dollars, Jimmy asked me three times, "Are you sure you will return the money to me?" Four days later, he kept reminding me about the loan until I paid him back the money.

Interestingly enough, weeks later he borrowed $30 from me and said he would pay me back in a week. After one month, there was no sign of the money so I reminded him. To my surprise, he said, "I'm sorry, why didn't you remind me earlier?" and returned the money instantly.

Americans don't readily give money to others nor receive others' readily. If you lent money to an American generously, and said, "Don't mention it again. You don't have to pay me back", he would be angry and think you were looking down on him, not believing his ability to repay the money.

Question

If you were "I" in this case, how would you adjust yourself?

Case two

In America, a Chinese overseas student came to a restaurant for a part-time job. The restaurant owner promised him that he could work here as a take-out deliverer under the premise that he had a car or bicycle. The student thought it not worth buying a bicycle or a car just for this job. He insisted that the owner should offer a bicycle for him. Finally, he had to give up the opportunity.

Another overseas student, once coming to America, used up the money from his pocket to buy a second-hand old car. With this car, he got several part-time jobs in different restaurants, and several months later, he changed a new car with the money he earned.

Question

How do you think of spending and saving in the above case?

3.5.2 The Different Concepts of Saving and Spending

In Chinese Culture, the personal savings rate in China is incredibly high compared to that of the United States. According to a 2006 CNN article, the personal savings rate of Chinese households is 30% while Americans dipped into their savings that year. Many Chinese regularly save 50% to 60% of their income and they feel this is the primary way of becoming rich.

In American Culture, Americans believe that God helps those who help themselves. Therefore, the consumption culture of Americans differs greatly from that of Chinese. They prefer spending money to saving, for the reason that they believe they can earn more to plow back what they have spent. Moreover, many Americans choose payment by installments, because "spend more, and earn more" is the concept as part of the culture that has deeply rooted in their minds.

For American Way of Saving, Americans have their particular way of saving money instead of just not spending it. Students studying in the US could find some practical methods of saving that are typical in American culture. The following are some recommendations: 1) make use of the various sales ads on campus, such as Church Sale, Estate Sale, Families Sale, Garage Sale, Moving Sale, Porch Sale, and Yard Sale; 2) drive to the flea market nearby; 3) move to the sublet during the holidays; 4) be informed of the preferential treatment by the local government to international students; 5) take advantage of the full refund policy of campus bookstores; 6) buying round-trip tickets is always cheaper than one-way tickets.

3.5.3 Asking for Salary and Price

One's salary is regarded as extremely personal and private in the West. Even within families, people often do not know the exact salary of other family members. This does not mean that the family is not close. It is better to avoid questions like "How much do you earn?" It is also very common in China to ask someone how much they paid for a particular item. In the West, although people may discuss price in general, it is not normally acceptable to ask someone directly how much they paid for something. The following illustrates a possible approach:

Xiao He: That's a beautiful plant stand! Where did you buy it?

Jennifer: At the plant shop on Siming Road.

Xiao He: Oh, I'd love to buy one myself. Was it very expensive?

Jennifer: Not really. In fact, I thought it was quite reasonable. I paid five yuan for it.

3.6 Modesty

Modesty is one of the traditional virtues the great sage Confucius advocated. Although a great scholar, Confucius admonished his students, "When walking in the company of three, there must be one I can learn from". To Confucius modesty and humility are required qualities for a society to sustain itself while pride will lead to destruction.

Daily Verbal Intercultural Communication

The typical example of modesty is demonstrated by the hosts to their visitors. The hosts will apologize for the ill-preparation and small quantity of his food, which turns out to be sumptuous banquet. And modesty is also shown when Chinese accept compliments. They always respond to compliments with "Nali, nali" (literally where, where?), which figuratively means "I have done nothing to deserve your compliment."

Another common way to show the Chinese modesty is that Chinese often politely refuse offers of drinks, refreshments, gifts and other favors two or three times before graciously accepting them. Their modesty requires them not to open the gifts before the sender.

Their modesty requires them not to challenge but to respect, which results in a low profile of Chinese. This is sometimes misunderstood as no confidence or competitive spirit. Their modesty leads them more to group-consciousness rather than to individual-consciousness.

Case Discussion

Case one

W: (Showing C the sofa) Sit down, please.
C: No, no. I will sit here. (Moving towards a chair)
W: Oh, do sit over here on the sofa.
C: No, no. This chair is perfectly all right.

Question

Could the Westerners understand Chinese's modesty to the host?

Case two

One day, Li Hongzhang was hosting a banquet for the American officials in a popular restaurant. As the banquet started, according to the Chinese custom, Li stood up and said, "I am very happy to have all of you here today. Although these dishes are coarse and not delicious and good enough to show my respect for you, I hope you will enjoy them..." (今天承蒙各位光临,不胜荣幸。我们略备粗馔,聊表寸心,没有什么可口的东西,不成敬意,请大家多多包涵……)

The next day, the English version of his words was shown in the local newspaper. To his shock, the restaurant owner flew into a range. He thought it was an insult to his restaurant and insisted that Li should show him the evidence of which dish was not well-made and which dish was not delicious. Otherwise, Li intentionally damaged the reputation of the restaurant, and he should apologize. All the fuss made Li rather embarrassed.

Question

What are the reasons accounting for Li Hongzhang's embarrassment?

3.7 Compliments

Compliments and complimenting response are an essential part of daily verbal communication. Various expressions of compliments and complimenting response manifest the cultural variations and different cultural roots. In the following, we are to introduce briefly the differences between Chinese compliments and English compliments. As far as the semantic formula and syntactic formula are concerned, common response formulas in English and Chinese, and the social functions of compliments are also discussed.

3.7.1 Case Discussion

Case one

A young Chinese woman who was new in the U. S. was complimented for the lovely dress she was wearing. "It's exquisite. The colors are so beautiful!"

Questions

1. How do you think she responded?
2. What would an American woman respond?

Case two

A Canadian woman acquaintance of a Chinese art teacher asked him to look over an article that she had written about Chinese painting. He agreed, but added something politely.

Question

What do you think he would like to add?

Case three

A famous Chinese actress married a German. One day when she was acting, her husband was there watching, saying again and again that she was the best actress. The actress' colleagues present asked her afterwards to tell her husband not to praise his own wife like that in public. On learning this, the German wondered what he did wrong.

When the actress and her husband were talking with their Chinese friends at a party, the husband politely praised a Chinese lady on her beauty. The lady's husband said that his wife was moderately good looking when young, but now she was old and no longer so. The lady nodded in agreement with a smile. The actress' husband was surprised.

Question

Explain why the German was confused in the first situation and surprised in the second.

3.7.2 Examples about Fishing for Compliments

- A: It's exquisite. The colors are so beautiful!
  B: Oh, it's just an ordinary dress I bought in China.
  Suspicion: But I think it is really nice.
  (A was forced to say so.)

- A foreign visitor was looking at the host's potted flowers with obvious admiration. The plants were blooming profusely. The host remarked diffidently, "Growing flowers is my hobby, but I'm not much good at it."
  Suspicion: "But these flowers are beautiful" or "I wish I could do as well!"
  (The visitor was forced to say so.)

- A Canadian asked a Chinese art teacher to look over an article that she had written about Chinese paintings. He agreed, but added that "I really know little about the subject."
  Suspicion: "Oh, come on. I know you're an expert on Chinese art." Or "Well, certainly don't know anybody who knows more than you do."
  (The Canadian was forced to say so.)

3.7.3 Proper Response to Compliments

- A: What a beautiful pen!
  B: It came from India. I went there on business last month.
  (Don't accept or refuse.)
- A: You're looking very smart today.
  B: Thank you. So are you.
  (Return the same compliment.)
- A: Your Japanese is very good.

B: Well, my listening isn't too bad, but I still have a lot of problems with speaking.
(Accept partly.)

- A: You look terrific today!
  B: Oh well, tomorrow I'll just go back to being myself.
  (Sometimes use self-effacing response.)
- A: You did a great job.
  B: Oh well, it had to happen sometime.
  (Sometimes use self-effacing response.)

3.7.4 Social Functions of Compliments

Compliments have a series of social functions:
- Creating or reinforcing solidarity;
- Greeting people;
- Expressing thanks or congratulations;
- Encouraging people;
- Softening criticism;
- Starting a conversation;
- Overcoming embarrassment.

Case one

(In formal situations) On behalf of all the American guests, I wish to thank you for the incomparable hospitality for which the Chinese people are justly famous throughout the world. I particularly want to pay tribute, not only to those who prepared the magnificent dinner, but also to those who have provided the splendid music. Never have I heard American music played better in a foreign land.

Question

Which social function of compliment can be reflected in the above case?

Case two

Situation 1: (In informal situations) A boss meets his young female employee in the morning.

A: Well, you look terrific in that dress!

B: Thank you. I have had this for a while.

A: Hi, Pat. How are you doing? You look nice.

B: Thanks, Anne. So do you.

Situation 2: Two acquaintances meet in the street.

A: Thanks for the Christmas present you sent me. It's so nice and just what I needed.

B: I'm glad you like it.

Situation 3: Two friends decide to make up after a quarrel. One comes to the apartment of the other.

A: Hi, Mary. How are you?

B: OK. How are you?

A: I'm fine. (pause)

B: Oh, this vase is really pretty. When did you get it?

Question

What social functions of compliments can be reflected in the above conversations?

3.8 Gratitude and Apology

If a teacher answered a question you asked, would you say "Thank you"? If your mother bought you a book that you needed, would you say "Thank you" to her? Explain why you would do so or not.

Some American tourists said "Thank you" to the interpreter who helped them during the tour and the interpreter replied, "It's my duty to do so." Although it is appropriate to say so in the Chinese context, is it appropriate in the English context?

Many Chinese often regard the frequent use of "Thank you" and "Please" by Westerners as unnecessary and even tiresome. On the other hand, Westerners sometimes take the Chinese attitude that appreciation is understood and need not be expressed for rudeness or lack of sincerity.

3.8.1 Expressions of Gratitude in English and Chinese

Examples on gratitude	Formulaic responses
Thanks.	Not at all.
Many thanks!	You're welcome.
Thanks a lot!	Don't mention it.
Thank you very much.	It's my/our pleasure.
Thank you very much indeed.	That's all right.
I greatly appreciate your timely help.	That's okay.
太谢谢(你)了。	不用谢。/谢什么。
很/十分/非常/万分感谢。	不客气。
麻烦辛苦您了。	这算不了什么。
您受累了。	这是我应该做的。

3.8.2 Expressions of Apology in English and Chinese

Examples on apology	Formulaic responses
Excuse me.	It doesn't matter at all.
I'm sorry.	Never mind (about that).
Sorry about that.	No harm done.
I'm very/so/terribly/awfully/extremely sorry for that.	No problem.
I can't tell you how sorry I am.	Forget it.
I beg your pardon for …	Please don't worry.
A thousand pardons for …	That's quite all right.
Please forgive me (for …).	I quite understand.
I must apologize for my rudeness/fault/mistake, etc.	There is no reason to apologize.
I apologize.	It's not your fault.
I must beg to apologize for …	Please don't blame yourself.
May I offer you my profoundest apologies?	It's really not necessary.
对不起。	没关系。
不好意思。	不要紧。
请原谅/谅解(我的过失/鲁莽/错误/粗心)。	没事。
我道歉。	不是你的过错。

Chapter Three
Daily Verbal Intercultural Communication

3.9 "No Politeness"

In the daily verbal communication, Chinese are honored as being polite in many ways. Politeness is deemed as a virtue in Chinese traditional culture. When encountering with Western culture, however, being polite is not always regarded positively. In the following three situations, Chinese don't have to show politeness in order to communicate well with Westerners.

Case Discussion

Case one

Having just recently arrived in Canada, I paid a visit to my boss. When I was leaving, to my bewilderment, the door was shut with a click the moment I stepped out of his house. I was upset about this for several days. Gradually, I came to know it was not only me who received such "treatment". When their boss or parents are leaving, the Canadians will not see them out of the door as well.

Questions

1. How do you think about no seeing out when guest leaves?
2. What are you supposed to do?

Case two

When my boss came into my office for the first time, I stood up immediately to show my respect. The boss misunderstood my behavior, thought I was going out, and said he would talk with me in a while. I was accustomed to respecting all those in authority. For instance, at an academic conference, if some academic experts came in late and unfortunately had to stand behind me, I would feel uncomfortable and offer my seat to him. On one occasion, I offered my seat to the head of the Department of Internal Medicine. He said "Thanks" and sat down. During the conference, he kept turning around and looking at me, which made me feel ill at ease. When the conference over, he came over and apologized to me, "I thought you were leaving the conference. You don't have to offer me."

Questions

1. How do you think about no stand-up when your leader comes in?
2. What are you supposed to do?

Case three

My landlady was over 70 and we got along very well. Once when we were ascending the stairs together, I stretched out my hands to give her some help. She said, "I can do it. Thank you." I thought she was just being polite, so I escorted her to the top floor. Her face showed that she could do nothing about my over-kindness. Soon after, I saw her going up the stairs alone; I forgot my previous lesson and did the same thing. This time, half-jokingly and half-seriously, she asked me, "Young man, do you think I am old and useless? When I have to move myself on a wheelchair, I'll ask you for help."

Questions

1. If you were the counselor of "I" in the case above, how would you help him?
2. How do you account for this phenomenon of no help for old people?

3.10 Visiting and Parting

Visiting and parting customs are especially important in daily verbal communication and show great differences between Western and Eastern cultures. If a visit is business rather than socially related, the Westerners prefer to arrange the time in advance, and care should be taken over the language used. Often Chinese make statement or command when they mean to make request, which is different from the Westerners in terms of the ways of making an appointment. Similarly, Parting can be a difficult task in any culture, and it will be particularly difficult for people in another culture. The guest has to decide how long it is appropriate to stay, and having decided to leave, needs to know what to say.

3.10.1 Case Discussion

Case one

Alice has a Western English teacher named Ms. Merrick. Several times on campus,

Daily Verbal Intercultural Communication

Alice has seen Ms. Merrick and chatted with her. At the end of conversations, Ms. Merrick often says, "Come over and visit me sometime." So, one evening Alice decides to go and visit.

When Alice finds Ms. Merrick's apartment, she knocks on the door. After a moment, Ms. Merrick opens the door, but she doesn't look very happy to see Alice. Instead of inviting Alice in, she says, "Can I do something for you?"

Question

Why does Ms. Merrick appear unhappy seeing Alice's visiting?

Case two

Jane, an American teacher, had just started teaching English to a group of Japanese students in the U. S. She wanted to get to know the students more informally, so she invited them to her house for a party. The students arrived together at exactly 8:00 pm. They seemed to enjoy the party: they danced, sang, and ate most of the food. At about 10:00 pm, one of the students said to the teacher, "I think it's time for me to leave. Thank you very much for the party." Then all the students stood up and left at the same time. Jane decided she would never invite them again.

Questions

1. Why did the Japanese students leave together at the same time?
2. How did the American teacher feel when all the students stood up and left at the same time?
3. Why did Jane decide never to invite the students to her house again?
4. What's the difference between the U. S. and Japanese in the notion of time?

Case three

When one of your colleagues or classmates is sick in hospital, will you go and visit him/her? If you do, will you give notice before you go? You are to read a story concerning hospital visiting. After reading it, try to explain why the visitors were upset and the patient and his wife were unhappy.

Jim had to have an emergency operation during his one-year teaching post in China. Starting from the next day after the operation, his Chinese colleagues went to the hospital to see him during visiting hours. To the discomfort of Jim and his wife, none of them gave any notice before their visit, and some came at inconvenient times. For the first three days, Jim had a hard time recovering from the operation, and his wife would stop the visitors at the door, and briefed them about how Jim was doing. But the visitors were very upset about not seeing Jim.

Questions

1. What were the visitors upset for?
2. Why were Jim and his wife unhappy?

3.10.2 Further Reading on Courtesy of Visiting and Parting

Before visiting, the Westerners prefer to arrange the time in advance. Making an appointment in advance is a basic politeness rule in Western countries. Generally, the Westerners are accustomed to doing one thing at a time and may be uncomfortable when an activity is interrupted. They are used to organizing and arranging their time. Visitors who "drop by" without prior notice may interrupt their host's personal time. Casual visiting is usually regarded as being impolite. Thus, making an appointment before visiting him or her is generally preferred to a "dropping by". So to accommodate other people's schedules, the Westerners make business and social engagements several days or weeks in advance.

The language used to make request of visiting should also be paid attention to. The following are some suitable expressions:

(1) I'd like to come and see you sometime. Would you be free one afternoon next week?

(2) I would like to come and visit you. Would it be convenient for me to come Wednesday evening?

(3) Mr. White and I would like to come and visit you. Would it be convenient for us to

come on next Friday evening?

(4) There's something I'd like to talk over with you. Would it be convenient to meet you this Friday afternoon?

(5) Shall we discuss the matter at 10 tomorrow morning? If not, please ring me to make another time—many thanks.

(6) Could we see each other for about an hour on Friday afternoon at three o'clock?

(7) I'm in town for a few days and would very much like to come and visit you at your house. Would it be convenient if I call on you this evening?

(8) I haven't seen you for a long time. I was wondering whether I could come round to visit you sometime.

After receiving an invitation, unequivocal reply should be given, for the Western custom is much stricter than Chinese custom in the matter of replying to invitations. When you receive an invitation you should answer it immediately, saying definitely whether you are able to accept it or not. If the invitation is given by word of mouth, in conversation or at a chance meeting, you should answer at once whether you can come or not. If you cannot give an answer at that time, you may say, "May I let you know this evening?" or some such words. Reply, like "I'll try to come." will cause to be perplexed or confounded.

When visiting, the most important thing is punctuality. Visitors must arrive at the meeting place according to the given time. Otherwise, the Westerners may feel slighted and get unhappy. If someone is unable to keep the appointment or wants to change the appointment because of some reason, he or she must notify the other party in advance and make an apology. Generally twenty four hours' notice is the absolute most polite time frame for cancellation of visiting without complaint.

During visiting, the Westerners often put things with them (such as out-door clothing, raingear, etc.) at the pointed place, sit down at the pointed sofa or chair. Then the host may offer something to drink like tea or coffee. They may take counsel with visitor like:

(1) How about a cap of tea?

(2) Would you like a cup of tea?

(3) Would you like some coffee?

(4) Would you like something to drink?

(5) Tea of coffee? Or something cold?

The responses can usually be "Yes. Please.", "Tea, please.", "No. Thank you." The visitors are expected to answer honestly, and if they say no, the host will not offer them any. Generally, the host doesn't repeat the offer more than once. If the visitors accept, they will be given a cup and expected to drink it all. Westerners tend to relate the meal size more accurately to the people's appetites; both the quantity and variety of the meal are far less than that in China. According to Western custom, "seeing the bottom" of all plates is the ideal ending to a meal, for it means that the guest has thoroughly enjoyed the meal. In the Westerner's opinion, it is bad manners to leave drinks in one's own cup or to leave food in one's own plate, and it may offend the host.

Chinese hospitality is extremely different when involving food. Chinese hosts usually prepare a sumptuous meal. Moreover, every time the visitor had nearly finished a dish, the hosts replenished it from the kitchen. In China "seeing the bottom" of a dish is a sign that the hosts have not prepared enough. They keep putting the best pieces of food on visitor's plate despite the fact the visitors may not like certain food, or they have had enough. This usually makes the Westerners feel very embarrassed. According to their culture they should finish eating all food on their plate. But the more they eat, the more they are given.

At the end of visiting, parting may be a difficult task in any culture. Two things often cause to be perplexed—"how long it is appropriate to stay" and "what it is appropriate to say".

After an hour or so of general chit-chat, it's probably time to head for the door. In Western culture, it is impolite to leave impulsively. Before leaving, visitors usually say something to imply preparing for leaving, but no immediate move to depart is actually made. At the same time the host may say something to urge the visitor to stay. Both continue their conversation or other shared activity for a while longer; this delay may last a couple of minutes.

The appropriate parting expressions in English:

(1) We have to say good-bye now. We enjoyed the evening very much. Thanks a lot.

(2) I think I'd better be leaving now. It's very nice to have a talk with you.

(3) It's been lovely to see you, but I must be going soon. I hope we'll be able to get together again before long.

(4) Thank you for a lovely afternoon. But I think it's time for me to leave now.

(5) I've very much enjoyed this afternoon. I'm afraid I must be going now.

The appropriate responses to parting expressions:

(1) Can't you stay any/a little/longer?

(2) Must you really be going?

(3) Do you really want to go?

(4) So soon? Can't you stay a little longer?

(5) Must you? It's still early.

In contrast with the Western culture, in China visitors often stand up suddenly and say, "得走了,我还有要紧的事" or "对不起,浪费了您这么多时间,我该走了", which seems quite abrupt, even impolite to the Westerners. At the mention of parting expressions, Chinese have its unique ones like: "请留步", "不要远送了". The host may say "请慢走", "请走好", "注意脚下", "有空再来". All of these can't be translated into English literally. According to Chinese culture, the host and the visitor exit from the door together and continue walking some distance while continuing to converse. The distance to which the host accompanies a guest is an indication of the esteem in which he or she is held. It is not uncommon for a host to accompany the guest down several flights of stairs and out of the building, or even to the bus stop before saying the final good-bye. As a general rule, Chinese prefer not to go back until the visitor is out of sight.

3.11 Common Topics in China and the West

Western ideas of privacy are somewhat different from those of the Chinese, thus the favorite topics among people in different cultures may vary sharply between Chinese and Westerners. Without an adequate knowledge of choosing appropriate topics, misunderstandings or even conflicts may easily occur during communication process.

3.11.1 Common Proper/Improper Topics in China

• Age, income, property, price, general questions about one's family life, especially children, sports, weather, news, traveling, interests and hobbies, politics and religion…

• Very intimate questions about one's family life, topics concerning death, addressing the senior's given name

3.11.2 Common Proper/Improper Topics in the West

• Weather, sports, news, work, traveling, interests and hobbies …

• Personal questions about age, weight, illness, income, property, religion and politics …

3.12 Review Tasks

Ⅰ. **Decide whether the following statements are true (T) or false (F).**

1. All cultures require and value politeness, but the ways in which politeness is achieved may vary significantly. ( )

2. The purpose of greeting is to exchange information. ( )

3. Chinese hospitality toward the Westerners is always greatly appreciated. ( )

4. The Chinese way of showing concern is usually appreciated by the Westerners. ( )

5. "Thank you for coming!" is a typical expression used by Western hosts when the guests just arrived. ( )

6. "I'm sorry to have wasted your time" or "I'm sorry to have taken up so much of your time" are usually appropriate for the business visit. ( )

7. Chinese people tend to say things like "No, not really" when they are asked "Are you hungry?" in the host's family. ( )

8. In American culture, modesty and humility are required qualities for a society to sustain itself. ( )

9. Sometimes the Chinese way of showing modesty may be considered as fishing for compliments. ( )

10. The social functions of Chinese and English compliments are roughly the same. ( )

11. Chinese people give more compliments in daily life than Americans. ( )

12. The cultural assumption of compliments is the same between cultures. ( )

13. Overcoming embarrassment is one of the social functions of compliments. ( )

14. Westerners take Chinese attitude that appreciation need not expressed for honesty and sincerity. ( )

15. As known in Western culture, people are expected to give an unequivocal reply after receiving an invitation. ( )

16. Topics such as age, income, or property are appropriate in Western culture. ( )

17. Americans tend to be self-effacing in their compliment responses. ( )

18. Compliments on other's belongings are sometimes an indirect way of request in American culture. ( )

19. If a guest compliments something in another person's home, the Chinese host or hostess will probably give that thing to the guest. ( )

20. For an important guest, the American host will see him or her to the building gate, or even to the bus stop. ( )

Ⅱ. **Discuss the following questions.**

1. What are the differences in showing hospitality in Chinese and Western cultures?

2. What is "No politeness"? Please summarize some situations in which people don't have to show politeness.

3. What topics should be avoided in initiating conversations?

Ⅲ. **Analyze the following cases and answer the questions.**

Case One

A Westerner invited a Chinese girl to have lunch and to take a tour around the British Parliament. In fact, the girl didn't have the lunch just because when the Westerner asked her "Are you hungry?" but the girl answered no. Then they didn't have lunch together. The second time, the girl was invited to a restaurant, when the host asked the same question "Are you hungry?" she answered "not really". The host ordered a light meal for her.

Questions

1. What are the misunderstandings in the above communication experience?

2. What can we learn from this case?

Case Two

Shao Bin, a Chinese student studying in Britain, was once invited by her British classmate Brain to his house to cook a Chinese meal. Her two Chinese friends were also invited. They busied themselves in the kitchen, making dumping while Brain did something in the garden and his wife sat on the sofa reading. Shao Bin felt a little upset for she thought that both the host and the hostess should offer to help with the kitchen work. The meal was great and everyone enjoyed themselves. The couple kept complimenting them on their cooking skills and asked for the recipe. But then after the meal, the couple just put down their chopsticks and started minding their own business, leaving the Chinese guests to clear the table and do the dishes. Shao Bin felt absolutely confused or even angry.

Questions

1. Why did Shao Bin feel confused and angry?
2. What should Shao Bin do in this situation?

Ⅳ. Extended Reading.

Gift-Giving Etiquette

We can seldom go wrong when we give gifts to others. In general, people love to give and receive gifts. They are reminders of pleasant times and friendship. But each country has its seasons and occasions for giving gifts. Gift-giving in some cultures is an art and is considered as an integral part of building intercultural professional and social relationships. We'd like to pay attention to the careful selection, wrapping of a gift and presenting it at the proper time and the proper place as well as with the proper manner.

To give the proper gift, one must understand the culture of the receiver. One man's meat can be another man's poison. Giving an inappropriate gift or one that is culturally insensitive can cause serious harm to a relationship—more harm than not giving any gift at all. However, one way to smooth out problems would be to learn about the intercultural gift-giving and gift-receiving rules.

When you're invited to someone's home or a social occasion, regardless of the culture, it is always appropriate to bring some sort of gift for the host or hostess. When giving your gift, you should know the specific superstitions and taboos in the culture. Be aware what gifts are appropriate. Generally speaking, it is better often bestow several inexpensive, well-thought-out gifts instead of lavish expenditures. Often the best gift is one representative of your country, something crafted only where you are from.

Of course, there are various differences concerning selecting, rapping, and presenting the gifts in various countries. The following text names just some gift-giving etiquette of a few typical countries.

1. China

General guidelines

Chinese people have their own culture when it comes to giving friends or relatives gifts. It is important to know that giving someone gifts should not be a one-way business. Courtesy requires reciprocity. The person who receives the gift should find a chance in the future to return the same favor by returning a gift of similar value the next time you meet. You can do simply by either paying a visit with a similar gift or by inviting the friend out for a meal with you paying the meal. Don't do it right on the next day because it may appear awkward.

Foreigners may find it awkward when your friend says "You don't need to buy anything when you come here", or "Keep it to yourself. I have a lot of these". He may not mean it. What you need to do is to insist on him receiving the gift since Chinese people do not tend to receive the gift immediately.

Don't mind it if he doesn't open your present immediately too. Chinese people would think opening the present in front of you would be impolite and so they would tend to put it aside and only open it after you have left.

Appreciated gifts

When it is a new-born baby, usually jade or silver bracelet or necklace should be good, particularly ones that can make the clinging sound so it will make some sound when the baby moves. Alternatively, some children's clothes, shoes or gloves would be good too. When it is an older child, some toys or stationary would be good.

When it comes to some old people, something practical should be considered. A walking-stick, some valuable food such as bird's nests or Chinese mushroom would be highly welcome. For those who go to visit their prospective parents-in-law, something more valuable would be an option, such as some good wine or something meaningful. If it is a family, a vase, some dining sets or paintings would be ideal. It is not easy to think of something special for every occasion. So very often if it is not of any special visits, some fruits such as apples or oranges would be good enough.

Gifts to avoid

There are also some taboos to avoid in Chinese culture. Though modern Chinese don't seem to mind them so much, it is still necessary to know what would be suitable in an occasion. Books would not be welcome in places like Hong Kong or Macao because the pronunciation of "book" in Cantonese resembles the sound of "loss". Especially for those people who are frequent players in race course or Mark six, they would definitely not welcome this idea.

Umbrellas would not be welcome in most places in China because the pronunciation of "umbrella" resembles separation. Of course nobody would like the idea of separation, particularly concerning your loved ones.

Clocks would not be welcome, particularly on someone's birthday because the pronunciation of "clock" resembles termination, which means death. No wonder people don't like receiving clocks as birthday gifts.

If you want to give your friends some fruits, remember to buy an even number of them because odd numbers would bring bad luck. So buy 10 apples instead of 9.

2. Japan
General guidelines

Gift-giving is an important part of Japanese business protocol. Moreover, gifts are exchanged among colleagues on July 15 and January 1 to commemorate midyear and the year's end respectively. It is a good policy to bring an assortment of gifts for your trip. This way, if you are unexpectedly presented with a gift, you will be able to reciprocate. The emphasis in Japanese business culture is on the ritual of gift-giving, rather the gift itself. For this reason, you may receive a gift that seems too modest, or conversely, extravagant. An expensive gift will not be perceived as a bribe.

A wrapped gift is often carried inside a shopping bag to avoid ostentation and minimize any hint that a gift is about to be presented. The best time to present a gift is toward the end of your visit. You can discreetly approach the recipient, indicating that you have a small gift. Avoid giving a gift early in a relationship or at any conspicuous moment. A gift for an individual should be given in private. If you are presenting a gift to a group of people, have all of the intended recipients assembled. Present gifts with both hands. It is customary to comment that the gift you are presenting, even if it is extravagant, is "an uninteresting or dull thing". This statement is meant to convey, "Our relationship is more important than this trivial items".

It is a mistake to give the same gift to two or more Japanese of unequal rank. People will also take offense if you are in the presence of a group of people and give a gift to one person, but fail to give one to the others who are present. Gifts are opened in private, because if the gift turns out to be a poor choice, "loss of face" will result. Also, if several gifts are presented to people of different status, opening them privately prevents any possible comparisons.

Before accepting a gift, it is polite to modestly refuse at least once or twice before finally accepting. Ensure that your gifts are wrapped. It's the safest to leave this task to a store or hotel gift-wrapping service.

The safest gift-wrapping choices are pastel-colored papers, without bows. Avoid wrapping gift with brightly covered papers or bows. If you are invited to a Japanese home, bring flowers (an uneven number), cakes or candy. If you receive a gift, be sure to reciprocate. Gifts in pairs are considered lucky.

Appreciated gifts
- foreign, prestigious name-brand items
- imported scotch, cognac, bourbon, brandy or fine wines (top-quality brands only)
- frozen steaks
- gourmet foodstuffs, fresh fruit
- electronic toys (if children are on your gift-list)
- cuff links
- pen and pencil sets
- something that reflects the interests and tastes of the recipient
- a simple commemorative photograph (i.e. taken from a gathering that the recipient attended)

Gifts to avoid
- Lilies, lotus blossoms, and camellias are associated with funerals. White flowers of any kind should be avoided. There is also a superstition that potted plants encourage sickness.
- Giving four or nine of anything is considered unlucky.
- Red Christmas cards should be avoided, since funeral notices are customarily printed in this color.

3. Germany

General guidelines

In Germany, a small gift is polite, especially when contacts are made for the first time. Substantial gifts are not usual, and certainly not before a deal has been reached if you don't want your intentions to be misinterpreted. Even small souvenir-style gifts to thank local staff for their assistance and hospitality during your stay at a company will not be expected but will always be appreciated. Avoid giving substantial gifts in private. The larger the gift is, the more official and public the giving should be.

Gifts are expected for social events, especially to express your thanks after you have been invited to a dinner party at a home. Avoid selecting anything obviously expensive, as this may make the other person feel "obligated" to your generosity. A lovely bouquet of flowers (though not red roses) for the lady of the house is typical gift. When purchasing this at the flower shop, ask the florist to wrap it up as a gift. Upon returning home, remember to send a hand-written thank you card to your hosts for their invitation.

Appreciated gifts

For the company you are visiting, quality pens, tasteful office items with your company logo, or imported liquor are usually safe choices. Fine chocolates can also be an appropriate gift when you are invited to a home. If you decide to bring alcohol, good imported liquor is the safest choice. You can also bring a wine of excellent vintage from your home country or an exceptional imported red wine. A gift of German wine, however, should then be a more up market label. If you are staying with a family, good gift selections can include coffee table book about your home country, or anything that reflects the interests of your hosts and is representative of your country. An elegant, tasteful silk scarf can be an acceptable gift for the lady of the house. A local food specialty of your home country is usually a good idea for a gift, provided it is not too exotic. Keep in mind that German tastes are generally on the conservative side, so especially for older hosts, very unusual food gifts may well be under-appreciated.

Gifts to avoid

Red roses are for lovers; lilies are used at funerals. A general rule would be to avoid including heather in a bouquet as it is commonly planted in cemeteries. Clothing, perfumes, and other toiletries are considered far too personal to be appropriate gifts. Scarves, however, are acceptable gifts according to German business protocol. Avoid bringing beer as a gift, since many of the finest brands in the world are already produced and widely available here.

4. United States

Selecting and presenting an appropriate business gift is a thoughtful gesture, but it is not expected.

Business gifts are often presented after the deal is closed. In most situations, gifts are those that come from your country. You may not receive a gift in return right away.

During the Holiday season (late November through the first week of January), gifts are exchanged. For your business associates, you can give gifts such as useful items for the office, liquor or wine. Choose gifts with no religious connotations (i. e. don't buy Christmas ornaments), unless you are certain of the religious background of your associates. While Christmas is the dominant celebration, and is widely commercialized during this period, people may be celebrating many other holidays during this period. Many stores and malls offer gift-wrapping services during the winter holidays.

When you visit a home, it is not necessary to bring a gift, although it is always appreciated. Flowers, a potted plant, or a bottle of wine are good gift choices. If you wish to give flowers, you can have them sent in advance to relieve your host or hostess from taking care of them when you arrive. If you stay in a US home for a few days, a gift is appropriate. You may also write a thank-you note.

Taking someone out for a meal or other entertainment is another popular gift.

Gifts for women such as perfume or clothing are usually inappropriate. They are considered too personal.

Gifts for children are often a thoughtful and appreciated gesture, but one should take into account the values of the parents. Many parents would object to your giving a toy gun or a violent video game to their child.

5. Saudi Arabia

Gifts should only be given to the most intimate friends. For a Saudi to receive a present from a lesser acquaintance is so embarrassing as to be offensive. It is not unheard of for an employee returning from leave to get the sack for the impertinence of bringing his boss a present from home. Even worse is expressing admiration for something belonging to another because it makes him feel obliged to make a gift of it. If one is confident enough and determined to give a gift, it must be the best affordable.

A carpet must, for example, be handmade even though most Saudis buy machine-made carpets for themselves. Never, however, buy gold jewellery or silk garments for men, as both are deemed in Islam. Platinum is most acceptable but, as it can be confused with white gold; silver is safer, provided it is properly hallmarked by a government authority (as opposed to merely bearing a maker's mark). As a gesture of respect, the recipient is likely to open and minutely examine the gift in the presence of the giver as well as any others who happen to be present. Nothing is worse than having him search in vain for a hallmark or, worse yet, turn a carpet over to find a loose weave or indistinct design on the reverse.

Owing to the extremely personal nature of giving gifts, traditional perfume is usually the most appreciated. Just as in Europe a man displays his status by his tailoring, so in Arabia he does so by his scent. The best quality costs well over £1,000 an ounce and the naive buyer can easily be deceived by synthetics which cheat him of his money and cause him to forfeit the esteem of the one to whom the scent is given. The same is true of incense, costing per kilogram roughly the same as an ounce of its extract. Before giving any scent, use it first and consider giving it only to those who express admiration for your taste.

Questions

1. What are general guidelines of intercultural gift-giving rules?
2. What are the most welcome gifts and what are taboo gifts in China?
3. How should we present a gift to a Japanese friend?
4. What kind of gifts are appropriate for a German friend?
5. What are proper gifts to an American host or hostess?
6. To whom people usually send gifts in Saudi Arabia?

Chapter Four

Non-verbal Intercultural Communication

> *Those who know do not talk. Those who talk do not know.*
>
> —Lao Zi
>
> *In human intercourse the tragedy begins not when there is misunderstanding about words, but when silence is not understood.*
>
> —Henry David Thoreau

4.1 Lead-in Cases

Case one

One British businessman is in Iran. After months of doing the right thing, such as building relationships with Iranian colleagues, respecting the influence of Islam on negotiations and avoiding any potentially explosive political small talk, the executive was elated when the formal contract was signed. He signed the papers and turned to give his Persian colleagues a big thumbs-up. Almost immediately there was a gasp and one Iranian executive left the room. The British executive didn't have a clue as to what was going on — and his Iranian hosts were too embarrassed to tell him.

The explanation was really quite simple. While the thumbs-up gesture means "good, great, well-played" in Britain, but in the Persian culture it is a sign of discontent and borders on the obscene. "I don't think I was ever more embarrassed in my life. I felt like a child who yells out a vulgar curse word without having any clue as to what it means," the executive says. "My colleagues accepted my plea of ignorance but the relationship was damaged. It wasn't that they thought I had truly meant the gesture as interpreted in their culture but rather that I was totally ignorant of it. I just never suspected there was anything wrong with it."

Questions

1. What does "the thumbs-up gesture" mean in China?
2. What does this story suggest to you?

Case two

When he visited the United States in 1959, the former Soviet Premier Nikita Khrushchev once used the clasped-hands-over-the-head gesture. The next day American newspapers printed it on first page, which shocked the whole country, and American people became indignant.

Question

What caused the indignation of the American people?

Case three

Edith, from the United States, is teaching English at a university in southern China. She is beautiful and well-educated, with M. A. Degree in literature. Xiao Chen, a high school graduate, is a tall policeman who knows very little English. Although Edith knows no Chinese at all, they came to know each other at a social gathering. Though they could not communicate verbally, they both felt a connection. And before long, Edith and Xiao Chen began dating. A few months later, they got married and moved to Boston, the United States. Xiao Chen could still only speak a little English.

Non-verbal Intercultural Communication

Questions

1. Is language communication necessary in making friends or finding lovers?
2. How could you interpret the case above?

4.2 What Is Non-verbal Intercultural Communication?

Nonverbal communication refers to all aspects of a message which are not conveyed by the literal meaning of words, including hand gestures, eye contact, posture and stance, facial expressions, odors, clothing, hair style, walking behavior, interpersonal distance, touching, architecture, artifacts, graphic symbols, preference for specific tastes, vocal signs, synchronization of speech and movement, time symbolism, and silence (Condon & Youself, 1975). Definitions of nonverbal communication differ from one expert to another. Generally speaking, it refers to communication without the use of words.

4.3 Functions and Significance

There are several main functions that can be attributed to nonverbal communication across cultures. The functions of nonverbal communication could be identified in the following five aspects: repeating, complementing, substituting, regulating and contradicting.

1. Repeating

People often use nonverbal messages to repeat a point they are trying to make. For example, if someone asks us for direction, we might tell him or her "to go this way or that way". At the same time we repeat our instructions non-verbally by pointing at a certain direction.

2. Complementing

Closely related to repeating is complementing. For example, you can tell someone that you are pleased with his or her performance, but this message takes in extra meaning if you pat the person on the shoulder at the same time. Physical contact places another layer of meaning on what is being said.

3. Substituting

We use nonverbal messages to substitute for verbal messages. If it is noisy at a big meeting, the speaker may stop for a few seconds as an alternative to say, "Please calm down so that I can speak." Instead of raising your voice by shouting after a great performance of the orchestra, you may silently sit there with an awed expression. Your expression automatically indicates that the performance is excellent and that you are moved by the experience.

4. Regulating

We often regulate and manage communication by using some form of nonverbal behavior. For example, a parent might engage in "stern" and direct eye contact with a child as a way of "telling" him or her to terminate the naughty behavior while guests are in the house. Hand clapping by the instructor in a classroom demands the attention of the students. Turn taking is largely governed by nonverbal signals. In short, your nonverbal behavior helps you control the situation.

5. Contradicting

On some occasions, nonverbal actions send signals opposite to the literal meanings contained in our verbal message. For example, you tell someone you are relaxed and at ease, yet your voice quavers and your hands shake. When you are sick and a friend asks you how you feel, you may say, "I'm fine" in weak voice and with a slouchy posture. Non-verbally, you are telling your friend that you are not fine, but verbally you give your friend an opposite answer. People rely mostly on nonverbal messages when they receive conflicting data like these, so we need to be aware of the dangers.

Discussion

Study the following situations and try to figure out the above-mentioned functions of the non-verbal communication.

(1) People in a group are boisterous and you might place your index finger to your lips as an alternative to saying, "Please calm down so that I can speak."

(2) You tell someone that you are pleased with his/her performance, and at the same time you pat the person on the shoulder.

(3) When we say "The new museum is in the south of that building", we usually point to a certain direction.

(4) Just before an important examination, you tell someone you are relaxed and at ease, but your voice is trembling.

(5) In conversation we nod our heads in agreement to indicate to our partners in communication that we agree and that they should continue talking.

4.4 Body Language

Body language is known as non-verbal behavior which transmits information through postures, gestures, actions and facial expressions. People communicate with each other by their body language in the ways of nodding, waving, eye contacting, shrugging and so on. These ways can sometimes express what the verbal language cannot express directly.

4.4.1 Gestures

Gestures are an important component of non-verbal communication. Some gestures have come to be widely accepted and understood, such as handshaking, a gesture that goes with greeting. But many gestures vary in meaning from culture to culture, as is illustrated by the clasped-hands-over-the-head gesture. What is acceptable in one culture may be completely unacceptable in another.

In China, holding up one's thumb means good, and raising one's little finger means bad. But Japanese will hold up their little fingers to express one is their lover. In America, waving one's hand means goodbye. But South Americans will not leave when they see this gesture; on the contrary, they will run towards you.

Americans often touch their temples to express somebody's cleverness. But this gesture means there is something wrong with one's mind or one is stupid to Chinese. Chinese are often surprised to see Americans lay their hands on the necks when they are full, because it is a suicide action to Chinese, who used to express fullness by patting their stomachs. For another example, people from English-speaking countries turn around their rings constantly to show nervousness or uneasiness. But if people in the mainland of China act like this, they will be regarded as showing off richness.

In Chinese culture, touching or pointing to one's own nose with raised forefinger signifies "It's me" or "I'm the one". In the Indian sub-continent, a woman sometimes uses the gesture of pointing her forefinger to her nose to express astonishment. In the Middle East, the same gesture stands for "at your service", and can be employed by either sex, but is used predominantly by men. In Iran the gesture that stands for "at your service" is to put the palm of one's right hand over one's right eye. Nodding by moving one's head up and down means a concurrence, a "yes", in India whereas the same gesture in Kuwait would mean the exact opposite, a dissent, a "no".

It is clear to see that the same gesture can have different meanings in different cultures, and people from different cultures will express the same meaning by different gestures. So it is necessary for us to know the cultural difference to avoid misunderstanding.

4.4.2 Case Discussion

Case one

Study the following gestures and try to figure out the meaning of each one in your culture.

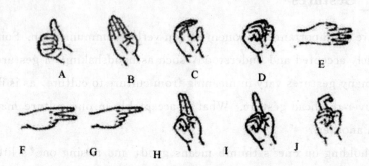

Case two

Two business people are sitting at a negotiation table. One is from Africa and the other is from Europe. The African businessman is putting his index finger to his temple which means he is thinking how to start negotiating with his counterpart. The gesture seems to have annoyed the European businessman, who has got impatient and stands up and shouts, "Why do you say at the beginning of our negotiation that I'm crazy?" The African, himself, is confused and at a loss as to what has gone wrong.

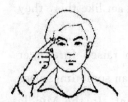

Question

Why is the African confused and what leads to their misunderstanding?

4.4.3 Postures

Posture communicates as a matter of how people sit, talk, stand and move. The way that people hold themselves gives important information and also offers insight into a culture's deep structure. The manner of sitting, standing and moving communicates a message and reflects a certain culture's lifestyle.

In many Asian cultures, a bow is much more than a greeting, and it signifies that culture's concern with status and rank. For example, in Japan the bow posture is an indicator of respect. The person who occupies the lower status begins the bow, and his or her bow must be deeper than the other person's. The superior, on the other hand, determines when the bowing is to end. When the participants are of the equal rank, they begin the bow in the same manner and end at the same time.

Non-verbal Intercultural Communication — Chapter Four

In the United States, where being casual and friendly is valued. People often fall into chairs or slouch when they stand. In many countries, such as Germany and Sweden, where lifestyles tend to be more formal, slouching is considered a sign of rudeness and poor manners.

According to Chinese tradition, people who are sitting have the right to take charge of others: monarch sits and officer stands; father sits and son stands; leader sits and employee stands and so on. So the younger give the old a seat to show respect. In America and Britain, however, people who are in charge of others have tendency to stand. They will make use of the height of space to indicate the high status. People who have high status choose to sit when they are conversing with you, which means they want to create harmonious and equal atmosphere and lessen space. So adults will bend down when they are talking to children.

4.4.4 Case Discussion

Case one

Once I went to an American bank to close my account before I left America. While talking with me, the bank manger put his feet with leather shoes onto the desk. When I returned home, I still could not forgive him for such behavior, thinking maybe he looked down on me because of my small savings or for being a Chinese. Later I came to know that an American's putting his feet on the desk shows that he is comfortable. However, for Latin Americans or Asians, such behavior is rude and arrogant.

Question

What made me misunderstand the American's behavior of putting his feet on the desk?

Case two

While lecturing to his poetry class at Ain Shams University in Cairo, a British professor became so relaxed that he leaned back in his chair and revealed the bottom of his foot to the astonished class. The next day the Cairo newspapers carried headlines about the student demonstration that resulted, and they denounced British arrogance and demanded that the professor be sent home.

Question

Why did the students become so angry?

4.4.5 Eye Contact

Eye contact is an important aspect of body language. In different cultures there have developed a variety of uses for the eyes in the communicative process.

People in Western societies expect the person with whom they are interacting to "look them in the eye". There is even a tendency to be suspicious of someone who does not follow the culturally prescribed rules for eye contact. Direct eye contact is not a custom throughout the world. In Japan, for example, prolonged eye contact is considered rude, threatening and disrespectful. People from Latin American and Caribbean cultures also avoid eye contact as a sign of respect. Problem can arise when Westerners attempt to do business with a group of people who believe it is a sign of impertinence to make prolonged eye contact with their communication partners. Arabs, on the other hand, look directly into the eyes of their communication partners, and do so for long periods. They believe such contacts show interest in the other person and help them assess the truthfulness of the other person's words.

4.4.6 Case Discussion

Case

A teenage Puerto Rican girl in a New York high school was taken by a number of other girls to the principal for suspected smoking. Questioned by the principal, the girl kept staring at the floor and refused to meet his eye. Although there was no proof of her wrongdoing and although she had a good record, the principal decided she was guilty and suspended her, basing his judgment on an English saying "Don't trust anyone who won't look you in the eye." "There was something sly and suspicious about her," he said in his report. "She just wouldn't meet my eye. She wouldn't look at me."

It's lucky that one of the teachers in the school had a Latin American background and he knew about Puerto Rican culture. He went to the principal and explained that according to Puerto Rican culture, a good girl does not meet the eyes of an adult. Such behavior, he

Non-verbal Intercultural Communication
Chapter Four

explained, is a sign of respect and obedience.

Fortunately, the principal accepted the explanation, admitted his mistake and the matter was settled promptly. This difference in interpreting eye contact was a lesson on cultural diversity that he would not easily forget.

Questions

1. Why did the principal believe that the girl was guilty at the beginning?
2. What can we learn from the principal's experience?

4.4.7 Facial Expressions

Human beings are animals full of emotions. Some psychologists believe that there are six basic emotions: surprise, fear, disgust, anger, happiness and sadness. Combinations of the six basic emotions give rise to others, such as embarrassment, shame, pride, shyness, boredom, suspicion and confusion, etc.

Our emotions are expressed both verbally and nonverbally. One of the nonverbal channels is facial expression on the look. The emotions expressed by one's looks carry other messages, like character and attitude as well as cultural connotation. In many Mediterranean cultures, people exaggerate signs of grief or sadness. It is quite common in this region of the world to see men crying in public. Yet in the United States, males often suppress these emotions. Japanese men even go so far as to hide expressions of anger, sorrow or disappointment by laughing or smiling. In one study, Japanese and American subjects revealed the same facial expressions when viewing a stress-inducing film while they were alone. However, when viewing the film in the presence of others, the Japanese manifested only neutral facial expression. The Chinese also do not readily show emotion for reasons that are rooted deeply in Chinese culture—the Chinese concept of "saving face" being one of the most important reasons.

4.4.8 Case Discussion

Case one

On the campus of a language institute in Beijing, there were overseas students studying English and Chinese. In 1989, a Japanese student, Sawada, came to the institute after studying two years in Australia. His English and Chinese were fairly good. One day, he met a girl on the campus from Holland, who introduced herself as Linda. Both of them were able to communicate in English. Sawada greeted her in Chinese, and Linda responded with a sweet smile and they began to talk in broken Chinese. As they were sitting on a bench, Linda turned her body toward Sawada and seemed to be very happy to have met this Japanese boy. As agreed, they met in Linda's apartment the following day to continue their talk. Observing that Linda was standing and sitting very close to him and looking at him with a sweet smile, Sawada felt she liked him, so he decided to put his arm around her shoulder. But to his disappointment, Linda pushed him away. Sawada thought she was shy, so he attempted a second approach by trying to hug her and kiss her. At this, Linda got very angry and asked him to leave the apartment. Sawada was quite puzzled and did not know why Linda refused him.

Question

Can you explain why Sawada was turned away? And why Sawada felt puzzled?

Case two

After living in the United States for more than a year, I am still puzzled by the fact that Americans can treat things so lightly. For example, after hearing my unpleasant experience, Americans might say, "That is too bad" with a smile on the face. I felt offended when I first saw the smile. I thought to myself, "Why didn't this person sympathize with me at all? How can he or she laugh at my misfortune?" What puzzled me more was that Americans talk about their own miserable experiences in a light way as well. One American woman casually told me about a vacation, saying, "After my dad passed away, my mother and I needed a break. He had been sick for years," and she smiled. I was shocked by her way of expressing relief. I decided Americans are very selfish and heartless because they could not have a serious face when they should be expressing sympathy or sorrow.

Non-verbal Intercultural Communication *Chapter Four*

Question

What made the author feel shocked, and what should be a right attitude towards this phenomenon?

4.5 Paralanguage

Everyone knows that the meaning of what we say is contained partly in the words, but that how we say things also contains powerful messages. The word "yes", for instance, may express defiance, resignation, acknowledgment, interest, enthusiasm or agreement according to the speaker's intonation, pitch and rhythm, depending on how it is said.

Paralanguage involves the vocal elements of speech; how something is said, not the actual meaning of the spoken words. It refers to the rate, pitch and volume qualities of the voice, which interrupt or temporarily take the place of speech and the meaning of a message. Vocal elements of language differ from verbal elements in that: vocal elements involve sound and its manipulation for certain desired or undesired effects. Verbal elements are the particular words we choose when speaking.

In most situations the classifications of paralanguage fall into three kinds of vocalization: vocal characterizers (laughing, crying, yelling, moaning, whining, belching, yawning), vocal qualifiers (volume, pitch, rhythm, tempo, resonance, tone), and vocal segregates ("uh-huh", "shh", "mmmh", "humm"). As silence also sends messages, it is usually included in the study of paralanguage.

In intercultural communication, misunderstanding caused by intonation, silence, volume, non-word noises may have as tragic consequences as misunderstanding of the meaning of the words actually used. For example, Americans and Chinese use very different ways in manipulating volume of speech. Liang Qichao, the famous reformist and scholar of the late Qing Dynasty, already noted in his book *Travels in the New World* that Americans were skilled in regulating their voice volume and they employed different volumes depending on the size of the audience and the physical environment, and his compatriots are lacking in comparable skills. Even to this day, this difference is still very striking. Silence is another example in voice modulation that indicates cultural divergence. It is interpreted as evidence of passivity, ignorance, apathy or hesitation in the American culture. Americans fail to appreciate Japanese speech habits, which view silence as necessary and desirable. They tend to think that there is no communication in silence. They try to fill in the pause in conversation, which fortunately can be misunderstood as pushy and noisy. To Japanese, silence is a rich communication style, which they regard as a virtue.

Case Discussion

Case one

In London's Heathrow Airport, airport staff who ate in the employees' cafeteria complained about rudeness by cafeteria employees from India and Pakistan who had been hired for jobs traditionally held by British women. And the Asian women complained of discrimination. A communication expert was asked to tape talk on the job to see what was going on, and then he had Asian and British employees listen to the tape together.

When a customer coming through the cafeteria line requested meat, the server had to find out if he wanted gravy on it. The British women asked, "Gravy?" the Asian women also said "Gravy". But instead of rising, their intonation fell at the end. During the workshop session, the Asian women said they couldn't see why they were getting negative reactions, since they were saying the same thing as the British women. But the British women pointed out that although they were saying the same word, they weren't saying the same meaning. "Gravy?" with question intonation means "Would you like gravy?" The same word spoken with falling intonation seems to mean, "This is gravy. Take it or leave it."

Questions

1. What made the Asian women feel that they were discriminated?
2. Why did the customers give negative reactions to the Asian women?

Case two

Vu Nguyen was a Vietnamese studying English in the United States. He often visited the local public library to read the magazines and newspapers. One day he found a book he wanted to read at home, so he asked the librarian, "Excuse me, may I borrow this book?"

The librarian answered, "Why, of course. Just give me your card."

Vu smiled at her and nodded his head politely. He wanted to show he was listening.

The librarian kept talking, "That book is wonderful. Isn't that author great?"

Vu had never read anything by the author. But he smiles and nodded again to show his interest. Finally, he said, "I would like to borrow this book today. Could you please tell me how to apply for a library card?"

Non-verbal Intercultural Communication

The librarian looked confused. "Oh, I thought you already had one. I'll give you a temporary card for today. We'll send you your regular card in the mail. It will be about two weeks. Come right this way to fill out the application." The librarian held out her hand, palm up, moving only her index finger to get Vu to follow her.

Now Vu was confused. He did not understand why the librarian had suddenly become so rude.

Vu smiled to cover up his confusion. As the librarian gave Vu the application, she said to him, "You look happy. You must be glad about your new library card."

Questions

1. In the case Vu's smiling and nodding just show his politeness and listening carefully, or means he had a library card?

2. How did the librarian understand Vu's smiling and nodding?

3. How did Vu think about the librarian's gesture (holding out her hand, palm up, moving only her index finger to get Vu to follow her)? What does this gesture mean in most Asian countries?

4.6 Time Language

Edward T. Hall pointed out, "Time talks. It speaks more plainly than words. The message it conveys comes through loud and clear. It can shout the truth where words lie." Each of us has the same amount of time every day, but time can be viewed and used in different ways.

Different cultures have different sense of time. There are three time orientations: past orientation, present orientation and future orientation. Some cultures tend to look back because they have a long history of which they can boast. They are past-oriented. Cultures that concentrate on the present and don't worry too much about tomorrow are present-oriented. Most post-industrial cultures are future-oriented because they place a lot of emphasis on the future, striving to ensure that the future will be better than the present.

Americans tend to be future-oriented. There are two reasons. Firstly, their ancestors served their links with their European roots and started anew. They do not have a long history, and do not like looking back on the past. Secondly, their values of independence and individualism drive them forward to build a brighter future.

Different cultures have different ways of organizing time. Hall (1976) elaborated on two time systems: Monochronic Time (M-Time) and Polychronic Time (P-Time). M-Time is noted for its emphasis on schedules, segmentation and promptness. It features one event at a time. Time is perceived as a linear structure just like a ribbon stretching from the past into the future. Northern American, Western and Northern European cultures are typical M-Time cultures. P-Time practiced by most other peoples is less rigid and clock-bound. People from P-Time cultures schedule several activities at the same time, and time for them is more flexible and more human-centered. Latin American, African, Arab and most Asian cultures are P-Time Cultures.

Chinese people in general belong to P-Time culture. Instead of tasks and schedules, human relationship is highly valued in China. There is an example showing how conflicts may arise if we are unconscious of these cultural differences. An American couple who has a lovely daughter teaches in a Chinese university, and many of their students like to go to their house to play with the little girl. The couple, although very friendly and hospital, sometimes feel unhappy, because the students often visit them during lunchtime without making appointments. This causes a lot of inconvenience to them. Therefore, in order to better communicate with people from other cultures, it is important for us to consider the different attitudes towards time.

 Case Discussion

Case one

Martha was an American high school student who was chosen to spend a summer in Indonesia as part of a student exchange program. When she got her letter of acceptance, she felt very lucky. She was sure that it was going to be the most exciting experience of her life. She did not even feel a bit sad about leaving her busy schedule back home: her piano lessons, the diving team, her church youth group and her baby-sitting job.

The first few days after her arrival in Indonesia were filled with meeting her new Indonesian exchange family, trying new foods, walking around the neighborhood, and getting to know her Indonesian exchange sister, Ketty. It was just as exciting as Martha had expected. But by about her second week in Indonesia, Martha began to feel as if something was wrong.

One morning, after breakfast, she looked at her watch and asked Ketty, "So what are the plans for today? What are we going to do?"

Ketty replied, "Oh, I didn't really make any plans. My mother might want us to go shopping with her later. Then we'll see what we feel like doing. Maybe we could go downtown."

Martha asked, "What time is your mom going shopping?"

Non-verbal Intercultural Communication

"Oh, whenever she's ready. Are you getting bored, Martha?"

"Oh, no, I guess I'm just used to being busy all the time. It's hard for me to get used to not having plans," said Martha.

"Doesn't bother you to rush around so much?" asked Ketty.

"No, I love it when I'm busy. Sitting around wasting time makes me nervous. Let's go to do something, Ketty. I'm only here for two months, after all. I don't want to leave Indonesia feeling that I haven't experienced as much as I can." Martha looked down at her watch again and said, "Goodness, it's almost 11 and all we've done is just sitting here and talking!"

Questions

1. What was Martha's life like at home?
2. Why did she begin to feel as if something was wrong?
3. What can you tell about the Indonesian concept of time?
4. What can you tell about Martha's concept of time?
5. What could make Martha feel better again?

Case two

Magid was an Arabian working in a company in the USA. One Sunday morning he was at home and didn't have much to do. He thought of his good friend, Jock, an American who he used to study with. They had not seen each other for a long time though they lived in the same city. And he had told Jock that he would come and visit him a long time ago. Now this Sunday morning seemed like a wonderful time for him to fulfill his visit. Without informing Jock of his visit, Magid went to Jock's house and rang the doorbell.

At the same time, Jock, after a whole busy week, was just looking forward to spending his Sunday reading and relaxing himself. Just as he started to read in his most comfortable chair, the doorbell rang. He opened the door and to his surprise, it was Magid who was standing at the door. He didn't look completely happy to see Magid. Then, after a few seconds, he smiled and said, "Hi, Magid. Come on in." They drank coffee and chatted about their life after their separation. Magid stayed about four hours and decided to leave. Jock walked Magid to the door. They said good-bye to each other and Jock thanked Magid for coming. After they left each other, both of them felt a little uncomfortable.

Questions

1. What didn't Jock look very happy to see Magid although they hadn't met for a long time?
2. Why did both of them feel a little uncomfortable after they left each other?
3. Can you give any advice to Magid before he visited Jock?

4.7 Space Language

The study of man's use of space is called proximics which is another silent language that people use to convey message. The study of proxemics is important in various fields, especially in business communication. According to Hall (1959), there are four major types of distances in American social and business circumstances: intimate distance (0-45 centimeters), personal distance (45-80 centimeters), social distance (1.30-3 meters), and public distance (farther than 2 or 3 meters).

Intimate distance is the closest distance often used in private situations. People who have a very close relationship, such as husbands and wives, lovers, and close family members, usually keep this distance. If someone is forced to be at this distance with a stranger in a crowded public situation, he/she would probably feel uncomfortable.

At personal distance, Americans usually hold conversations with friends, colleagues, and some members of their family. Actually, most of our everyday communication situations take place within this range.

Social distance is generally used for social gatherings and impersonal business. When an American student is in a class in which the teacher is leading a questions, he will most likely feel more comfortable within this range of distance from the teacher.

Public distance is the longest distance in interpersonal communication, including the space in which a person feels comfortable in a public area or gathering. The amount of this space will vary accordingly. It is appropriate for highly impersonal situations such as the movies, theater, lectures, or sports events, indicating that there is little or almost no personal relationship between them.

Generally speaking, people living in colder climates keep large physical distances when talking with others, whereas those from warm climates prefer close distances. Cultural values and thinking patterns also exert great influence on personal distance: cultures that stress individualism usually demand more space than collective cultures and tend to take an active, aggressive stance when their space is violated. However, due to the large population and limited public space, the idea of "personal space" is relatively weaker in China, and people sometimes seem insensitive to the accidental physical touch with strangers. Therefore, it is important for us to bear in mind that most English-speaking people do not like strangers to get too close; otherwise they will feel very uncomfortable. Violation of their personal space may cause misunderstanding in interpersonal communication.

Cultures can be reflected in seating arrangements. Americans tend to talk with those opposite them rather than those seated or standing beside them. This pattern also influences how they selected leaders when in groups: in most instances, the person sitting at the head of the table is chosen. In China, seating arrangements take on a different meaning. Facing someone directly or sitting on opposite sides of a desk or table makes Chinese feel as if they are on trial. In China, meetings often take place with people sitting next to each other.

 Case Discussion

Case one

When a North American and a Mexican stand together to converse, the Mexican will nudge slightly closer to the North American. The North American will step back an inch or two. Then the Mexican will move closer. These two will create a dance in which they will move across a considerable amount of space in the course of a brief conversation. If the space is crowded with people, they will end up moving around and around in a circle.

Question

How do you account for this?

Case two

During his stay in Japan, Boon, an American student, found that with exception of a few one- and two-room apartments, every house he ever visited in Japan was designed to incorporate three common elements: tatami, fusuma (sliding screens made of paper and light wood) and shoji (a type of even simpler sliding screen). It was not surprising to find certain similarities in the behavior and attitudes of the people who lived in them.

The most striking feature of the Japanese house was lack of privacy, the lack of individual, inviolable space. In winter, when the fusuma were kept closed, any sound above a whisper was clearly audible on the other side. There was no such a thing as the individual's private room, no bedroom, dining- or sitting-room, since in the traditional Japanese house there was no furniture determining that a room should be reserved for any particular function. A person slept in a room, for example, without thinking of it as a bedroom or as his room. In the morning his bedding would be rolled up and stored away in a cupboard; a small table known as the kotatsu, which could also be plugged into the mains to provide heating, was moved back into the center of the room and here the family ate, drank, worked and relaxed for the rest of the day. Although it is becoming standard practice in modern Japan for children to have their own rooms, many middle-aged and nearly all older Japanese still live in this way.

Questions

1. What cultural features are reflected in the interior design of a Japanese home?

2. Compare the Japanese house with the Chinese house. Are there any similarities and differences?

4.8 Review Tasks

Ⅰ. Decide whether the following statements are true (T) or false (F).

1. Speaking is just one mode of communication and there are many other nonverbal communication types.   (   )

2. In face-to-face communication, non-verbal signals are not as important as verbal messages.   (   )

3. Much of our nonverbal behavior, like culture, tends to be elusive, spontaneous and frequently goes beyond our awareness.   (   )

4. Nodding the head means "yes", and shaking the head means "no" in all cultures.   (   )

5. In American culture, people who are sitting have the right to take charge of others.   (   )

6. People from English-speaking countries turn around their rings constantly to show nervousness or uneasiness.   (   )

7. In most western countries, people pay less attention to their private space.   (   )

Non-verbal Intercultural Communication

8. Staring at people or holding a glance too long is considered to be improper in most English-speaking countries. ( )

9. In some cultures, eye contact should be avoided in order to show respect or obedience. ( )

10. Chinese don't readily show emotions mostly for the reason of "saving face". ( )

11. Paralanguage involves the actual meaning of the spoken words instead of how something is said. ( )

12. Silence is ambiguous, for it can be interpreted as agreement, disagreement, confusion, respect, sadness, and so on. ( )

13. Most South American countries belong to past-oriented cultures which emphasize current and short-term benefits. ( )

14. Latin American, African, Arab and most Asian cultures are M-Time cultures. ( )

15. The appropriateness of physical contact varies with different cultures. ( )

16. Social distance is the longest distance among four categories of interpersonal space, and can often be seen in some social gatherings and impersonal business. ( )

17. In intercultural communication, misunderstanding caused by intonation, silence, volume, etc may have the same tragic consequences with that caused by the meaning of words. ( )

18. Most of our everyday communication situations take place within social distance. ( )

19. Generally people living in colder climates keep large physical distances when talking with others. ( )

20. Chinese people tend to talk with those opposite them rather than those seated or standing beside them. ( )

II. Discuss the following questions.

1. What is nonverbal communication? What are the functions of it?
2. List some Chinese gestures that may be most probably misunderstood by Westerners.
3. What different messages do you think silence can communicate both in American and Japanese culture?

III. Analyze the following cases and answer the questions.

Case One

During his presidency, Bill Clinton traveled to China and, at one stop during the trip, spoke to university students in Beijing. His remarks were generally well received and were followed by a lively question and answer session.

When interviewed by an American reporter, one student remarked, "During the question and answer period, I did not understand why the President pointed his finger at us to select a person. We would not use such a rude gesture." Puzzled, the American reporter asked the student what gesture the President should have used.

Questions

1. What would you think was the gesture that the student recommends?
2. Can the gesture recommended by the student be applied universally? Why or why not?

Case Two

Several years ago, a popular American politician took a trip to Latin America. Upon his arrival at the airport, he emerged from the airplane, stood at the top of the loading ramp, and waved to the people awaiting his arrival. Someone shouted out, asking him how his trip was. He responded by flashing the common "OK" gesture. Shortly thereafter, he left the airplane and engaged in a short visit with a local political leader. Following that visit, he went to the major university in the area and delivered an address on behalf of the American people. During his talk, he emphasized that the United States was most interested in helping this neighboring country through economic aid that would help develop the economy and relieve the difficult economic surroundings of the poor. His speech, in fact, his entire visit was a disaster.

Questions

1. What does the "OK" gesture in Latin America mean?
2. Why was this American politician's visit a disaster?

Case three

Peter is a manager of a company in Japan. Recently, he made a mistake at work that caused some difficulties requiring a lot of effort to make up. Peter was very upset about what had happened, and came to the General Manager's office to make a formal apology.

Peter went into the Japanese General Manager's office after being told, smiling before he spoke. "I've been feeling very upset about the trouble I've caused for the company. I'm here to apologize for my mistake. I'm terribly sorry about it and I want you to know that it will never happen again." Peter said, looking at the Manager with the smile since he walked into the office.

The Manager found it hard to accept the apology. He looked at Peter and asked, "Are you sure?"

"Yes, I am very sorry and I promised this won't happen again." Peter said, with a smile even broader than before.

"I'm sorry I just can't take your apology. You don't look sorry at all!" the Manager said angrily.

Peter's face turned very red. He did not in the least expect the Manager to take it negatively. It was desperate to make himself understood. But he managed to smile again, "Please, trust me. No one can feel any sorrier than I do about it."

The Manager was almost furious by now, "If you're that sorry, how can you still smile?"

Questions

1. Why was the General Manager so angry about Peter's sincere apology?
2. What do you think of Peter's smile when he said sorry to the Manager?

Ⅳ. Extended Reading.

"Getting Real"
—Teachers and Immediacy Behaviors

A considerable amount of research has been done on teachers' use of immediacy behaviors, which points to the importance of this communication concept in teaching professions. Immediacy behaviors are verbal and nonverbal behaviors that lessen real or perceived physical and psychological distance between communicators. Specific nonverbal behaviors have been found to increase or decrease perceived levels of immediacy, and such behaviors impact student learning, teacher's evaluations, and the teacher-student relationship. Even those who do not plan on going into teaching as a career can benefit from learning about immediacy behaviors, as they can also be used productively in other interpersonal contexts such as between a manager and employee, a salesperson and a client, or a politician and constituent. Much of this research in teaching contexts has focused on the relationship between immediacy behaviors and student learning, and research consistently shows that effective use of immediacy behaviors increases learning in various contexts and at various levels. Aside from enhancing student learning, the effective use of immediacy behaviors also leads to better evaluations by students, which can have a direct impact on a teacher's career. While student's evaluations of teachers take various factors into consideration, judgments of personality may be formed after only brief initial impressions. Research shows that students make character assumptions about teachers after only brief exposure to their nonverbal behaviors. Based on nonverbal cues such as frowning, head nodding, pointing, sitting, smiling, standing, strong gestures, weak gestures, and walking, students may or may not evaluate a teacher as open, attentive, confident, dominant, honest, likable, anxious, professional, supportive, or enthusiastic. The following are examples of immediacy behaviors that can be effectively used by teachers:

(1) Moving around the classroom during class activities, lectures, and questions (reduces physical distance).

(2) Keeping the line of sight open between the teacher's body and the students by avoiding or only briefly standing behind lecterns / computer tables or sitting behind a desk while directly interacting with students (reduces physical distance).

(3) Being expressive and animated with facial expressions, gestures, and voice (demonstrates enthusiasm).

(4) Smiling (creates a positive and open climate).

(5) Making frequent eye contact with students (communicates attentiveness and interest).

(6) Calling students by name (reduces perceived psychological distance).

(7) Making appropriate self-disclosures to students about personal thoughts, feelings, or experiences (reduces perceived psychological distance, creates open climate).

Teachers who are judged as less immediate are more likely to sit, touch their heads, shake instead of nodding their heads, use sarcasm, avoid eye contact, and use less expressive nonverbal behaviors. Finally, immediacy behaviors affect the teacher-student relationship. Immediacy behaviors help establish rapport, which is a personal connection that increases students' investment in the class and material, increases motivation, increases communication between teacher and student, increases liking, creates a sense of mutual respect, reduces challenging behavior by students, and reduces anxiety.

(*Adapted from http://2012books.lardbucket.org*)

Questions

1. What are the benefits of the effective use of immediacy behaviors in teaching context?
2. What can be manifested when teachers are judged as less immediate?

Chapter Five

Interpersonal Relationships

> *Communication between men and women can be like cross-cultural communication, prey to a clash of conversational styles.*
>
> —*Deborah Tannen*
>
> *I don't need a friend who changes when I change and who nods when I nod; my shadow does that much better.*
>
> —*Plutarch*
>
> *All human beings have social needs which cannot be satisfied except in association with their fellow human beings.*
>
> —*Francis L. K. Hsu*

Personal relationships are universally important. As nobody is culturally free, people of different cultural backgrounds carry different expectations about relationships. The problem is that most of them expect people everywhere to develop relationships in similar ways. This is where misunderstanding and even conflicts may arise. Communication will then be affected.

Among various aspects of interpersonal relationships, we will focus on four sets of relationships that every one of us is involved in: cross-gender relationship, family relationship, friendship and I/C theory. These four types of relationships are closely interrelated, which influence every aspect of our daily lives. However, the manners in which people are related are not the same in different cultural contexts.

5.1 Understanding Cross-gender Communication

5.1.1 Lead-in Cases

Case one

John, 28 years old, an Australian studying Chinese in Beijing, met Li Hua at a dance party. Li Hua, 22, took an instant liking to John the first time they met. As time went on, they saw more and more of each other. After six months or so, Li Hua suggested that John meet her parents. Since this was the first time John had visited a Chinese family, he became quite nervous when he was introduced to Li Hua's parents, elder sister and sister-in-law. Soon after serving him some Chinese tea and fruit, Li Hua's mother began questioning John about his background, his family and relatives, as well as his economic status. John did his best to answer all of the questions, sometimes in broken Chinese. A few minutes later, Li Hua's father turned toward John, and asked a very direct question. He wanted John to tell him when he would marry Li Hua and where he was going to live and work. John, being a bit surprised at the question, replied that he hadn't thought about marriage. Li Hua's father got very upset and angry. He stamped his foot and asked John to leave. As John was about to leave, Li Hua's father warned him against seeing his daughter again. John left, without knowing what he had done to enrage the family.

Questions

1. How could you explain to Li Hua's parents about the relationship between Li Hua and John?
2. How could you explain to John about Li Hua's parents' behavior?

Case two

Anna asks her fiancé, Ben, "Can we talk about us?" Immediately Ben tenses up, sensing trouble. He prepares himself for an unpleasant conversation and reluctantly agrees. Anna then thanks Ben for being so supportive during the last few months when she was under enormous pressure at her job. She tells him she feel closer than ever to him. Then she invites Ben to tell her what makes him feel loved and close to her. Although Ben is relieved to learn there is no crisis, he's also baffled: "If there isn't a problem, why do women need to talk about the relationship? If it's working, let it be."

Interpersonal Relationships — Chapter Five

Question

Could you explain why Ben was reluctant to have a talk with his fiancée?

Case three

Chen Hua pursued an MA program at a university in Boston, the U. S. One day after class, his American friend, James, asked Chen to join him in the university cafeteria. On their way they ran into James' girlfriend, Lisa. Walking shoulder to shoulder, James and Lisa carried on an intimate conversation, as if they hadn't seen each other for ages. Meanwhile, Chen was walking behind them, not taking part in the conversation. When they were nearing the cafeteria Lisa said she had to leave for the lecture. James embraced her and gave her a long and passionate kiss. Seeing this, Chen turned away and walked off toward the cafeteria. When James looked up, he saw Chen walking into the cafeteria. James was puzzled as to why Chen didn't wait for him, and went to the cafeteria alone.

Question

Could you explain to James why Chen walked into the cafeteria without waiting for him?

5.1.2 Sex and Gender

What is sex? What is gender? Sex is determined by genetic codes that program biological features. The words like "man", "woman", "male" and "female" indicate sexual identities. Gender is more complex than sex. For example, you might think of gender as the cultural meaning of sex. Since the first cry in this world, individuals are besieged with communications reflecting cultural prescriptions for gender. Gender socialization continues with interactions between parents, teachers, peers, and the media. Through our interactions with others, we receive constant messages that reinforce females' conformity to femininity and males' to masculinity. For instance, parents may say to their daughter who are jumping and laughing too boisterously, "Behave like a girl!", while they may tell their crying son, "Be a man. No tears!" This means that individuals are not born with a gender, but are gendered. Although some people resist gender socialization, the intensity and pervasiveness of social prescriptions for gender ensure most females will become feminine and most males will become masculine. So gender is a social creation, not an individual characteristic. Everyone is consciously or unconsciously gendered the minute he or she comes into the world.

Sex	Gender
biological	socially-constructed
permanent	varied over time and across cultures
with an individual property	
with a social and relational quality	

In all, gender and sex are not synonymous. Sex is determined by genetics and biology, while gender is produced and reproduced by society. Societies create meanings of gender; in turn, individuals become gendered as they embody social prescriptions in their personal identities.

5.1.3 Differences between Feminine and Masculine Communication Cultures

- **Feminine Talk (1 – 10 items)**

1. Use talk to build and sustain rapport with others.

2. Share aspects about yourself and learn about others through disclosure.

3. Use talk to create symmetry or equality between people.

4. Matching experiences with others shows understanding and empathy.

5. To support others by expressing an understanding or their feelings.

6. Include others in conversation by asking their opinions and encouraging them to elaborate. Waiting one's turn to speak so others can participate.

7. Keep the conversations going by asking questions and showing interest in other's ideas.

8. Be responsive. Let others know you hear and care about what they say.

9. Be tentative so that others feel free to add their ideas.

10. Talking creates human relationships in which details and interesting comments can enhance the connection.

- **Masculine Talk (1 – 10 items)**

1. Use talk to assert yourself and your ideas.

2. Avoid personal disclosures that can make you vulnerable.

3. Use talk to establish your status and power.

4. Matching experiences is a competitive strategy to command attention.

5. To support others, do something helpful—give advice or solve a problem for them.

6. Don't share the talk stage with others. Interrupt others to make your own points.

7. Each person is on his or her own; it is not your responsibility to help others join in.

8. Use responses to make your own points and to outshine others.

Interpersonal Relationships   Chapter Five

9. Be assertive so others perceive you as confident and in command.

10. Talking is a linear sequence that should convey information and accomplish goals. Extraneous details get in the way and achieve nothing.

5.1.4 Case Discussion

Case one   Supporting

Rita is very bummed out when she meets Mike for dinner. She explains that she's worried about a friend who has begun drinking heavily. When Mike suggests she gets her friend counseling, Rita repeats how worried she feels. Mike tells Rita to make sure her friend doesn't drive after drinking. At this point Rita explodes, saying that she doesn't need his advice. Irritated at her lack of appreciation for his help, Mike asks, "Then why did you ask for it?" Exasperated, Rita responds, "Oh, never mind. I'll talk to Betsy. At least she cares how I feel."

Question

What counts as support from the above case?

Case two   Tricky Feedback

Roseanne and Drew are colleagues in a marketing firm. One morning Drew drops into Roseanne's office to discuss advertising with her. As Drew presents his ideas, Roseanne nods and say "Um", "Uh huh" and "Yes". When he finishes and asks what she thinks, Roseanne say, "I really don't think that plan will sell the product." Feeling misled, Drew demands, "Then why do you agree the whole time I presented my idea?" Completely confused, Roseanne responds, "What makes you think I was agreeing with you?"

Question

How do you think about Roseanne's "tricky feedback"?

Case three Expressing Love

Dedrick and Melita have been dating seriously for two years. To celebrate their anniversary Melita wants to spend a quiet evening in her apartment where they can talk about the relationship and be alone with each other. When Dedrick arrives, he's planned to dine out and go to a concert. Melita feels hurt because she thinks that he doesn't want to talk and spend the evening alone with her.

Question

How do you explain their different plans for the anniversary?

Case four By Myself

Jay is having difficulty in writing a paper for his communication class, because he's not sure what the professor wants. When he mentions this to his friend Ellen, she suggests he ask the professor or a classmate to clarify directions. Jay resists, saying "I can figure it out on my own."

Question

How do you understand Jay's reply?

5.1.5 Extended Reading on Cross-gender Communication

Six Principles of Effective Cross-gender Communication

We are inclined to think what differs from our own standards as wrong. For example, a woman might assume a man is closed because he doesn't disclose as much as she does, while a man might regard a woman intrusive if she cares too much about his feeling. Instead of debating which is better, either feminine or masculine style of communication, we should learn to see difference as mere difference. The following six principles are constructive in achieving effective cross-gender communication.

(1) Suspend judgment. This is first and foremost, because as long as we are judging differences, we are not respecting them. When you find yourself confused in cross-gender conversations, resist the tendency to judge. Instead, explore constructively what is happening and how you and your partner might better understand each others.

(2) Recognize the validity of different communication styles. In cross-gender communication, we need to remind ourselves that there is a logic and validity to both feminine and masculine communication style. It is inappropriate to apply a single criterion—either masculine or feminine—to both gender's communication. Instead, we need to realize that different goals, priorities, and standards pertain to each.

(3) Provide translation cues. Now that you realize men and women tend to learn and apply different rules for interaction, it makes sense to think about helping the other gender understand your communication. For instance, in the first case, Rita might have said to Mike. "I appreciate your advice, but what I really need is for you to recognize my feelings." A comment such as this helps Mike interpret Rita's motives and needs. After all, there is no reason why Mike should automatically understand rules that are not a part of his gender culture.

(4) Seek translation cues. We can also improve our interactions by seeking translation cues from others. In the case discussion, if Rita did not tell Mike how to understand her, he could have asked, "How can I help you? I don't know whether you want to talk about how you are feeling or how to help your friend, which could be better." This message communicates clearly that Mike cares about Rita and he wants to support her if she'll just tell him how. Similarly, in the second case instead of blowing up when Roseanne disagreed with him and assuming she had deliberately misled him, Drew might have taken a more constructive approach and said, "I thought your feedback during my explanation indicated you agreed with what I was saying. What did it mean?" This kind of response would give the opportunity for Drew to learn something new.

(5) Enlarge your own communication style. Studying other culture's communication teaches us not only about other cultures, but also about ourselves. If we are open to learning and growing, we can improve out own communication skills. Men could learn a great deal from feminine communication style about how to support. Similarly, women could expand the ways they experience intimacy by appreciating "closeness in doing". There is little to risk and much to gain by incorporating additional skills into our personal repertoire.

(6) Suspend judgment. If you are thinking we already covered this principle, you are right. It is important enough, however, to merit repetition. Judgment is so thoroughly woven into western culture as well as Eastern culture that it is difficult not to evaluate other and difficult to resist our own positions. Yet as long as we judge others and defend ourselves, we are probably making no advancement in communicating more effectively.

Therefore, suspending judgment is the first and last principle of effective cross-gender communication.

(Adapted from Gender, communication, and Culture by Julia T. Wood)

5.2 Family Relationship

5.2.1 Lead-in Cases

Case one

Emma felt worried these days. She lived with her parents-in-law in China. A year ago, she married Chen and came to China from America with her husband. They loved each other very much and she thought she would have a good relationship with her parents-in-law. However, she found it was becoming difficult now. Her mother-in-law had given too much advice on her matters. She often had to give up her own idea to obey, or her mother-in-law would feel unhappy. This also influenced the relationship between her husband and her. She wanted him to stand by her side, but he did not.

Questions

1. What is the problem that Emma was facing?
2. Could you give your advice to solve this family relationship problem?

Case two

The following two pictures represent two types of family. Can you tell which type each belongs to? Are there other types of family that you know of? Discuss with your classmates and try to list some.

Interpersonal Relationships　　　Chapter Five

5.2.2　Classification of Family Structures

Family is where people get their start in life. It is among the oldest and most fundamental of all human institutions. Different countries cultivate different family values. China and the United States, for example, have shown much difference in family structures and values.

Families can be divided, on the basis of generations, into *extended families* in which three or more generations live together and *nuclear families* in which there are only parents and children. But in recent years in some countries, Western ones in particular, definitions of family have begun to include different configurations: *live-in* couples, heterosexual or homosexual, with or without children, who are unmarried but have a binding relationship, *single-parent families*, in which the parent—married, never married, widowed, or divorced—lives with their biological or adopted children; *blended families*, consisting of two adults and their children, all, some, or none of whom may be the offspring from their union; and *DINK families*, meaning "double-income-no-kid" families.

5.2.3　Family Relationship Patterns

1. The older parents and the family

In traditional Chinese family, elderly parents usually live with their children and help them raise the grandchildren, while the young parents work hard outside to support the family financially. However, most elderly Americans, who rely on their own pension, live alone in retirement houses or "old folk's home".

Case Discussion

Professor Zhu Yongtao tells a story in his book *American Values of an Old Chinese Lady in America*. She lived with the family of her daughter and her son-in-law who is an American, looking after her grandson. One day she felt seriously ill and needed an operation. Hospitalization expenses were high and she had no medical insurance. The husband said to his wife, "We could not afford the expenses." Extremely surprised and angry, the wife told him that she would save her mother even at the cost of her own life.

Questions

1. Why did the husband say in that way?

2. Why did the wife react so strongly after hearing what her husband had said?

2. Husband and wife

"The husband doctrine" is the characteristic of Chinese traditional thought. In the traditional China, wives are taught to assume all obligations and liabilities from the loyalty to her husband. Today, the equality between men and women is not fully realized. For example, the wife needs to balance work and family, and take more care of the family. Besides, the wife needs to undertake more housework than the husband.

Americans put more emphasis on equality and liberty in the relationship between husband and wife, emphasizing the couples have equal status in the family, and also bear the same obligations and responsibilities.

Husband and wife share housework and enjoy family outcomes, for example, tending children together, spending more private time with family members, including annual travel plans.

Case Discussion

An American young man loved a Chinese girl. They married soon. At last the Chinese girl resigned her desirable position, and went to America with the American young man.

"I gave up a good job, and went far away from my hometown. I do all these just because of you. This is my contribution," said the Chinese girl. But the American young man argued, "Oh, no. I don't think this is one kind of contribution. In my opinion, this is just a choice. If you feel happy, and think your choice is correct, everything is all right."

Shortly after that, the Chinese girl said to her husband once more, "I had an excellent major before, but now I should spend so much time in studying a new major. I wasted so much time. Is it one kind of contribution?"

Beyond her expectation, the American husband said, "Please, don't always mention contribution. Everyone should be responsible for her choice. Now that you think your choice is valuable, this choice is correct, and you'll feel happy about it."

Questions

1. Can you explain the misunderstanding between this young couple?

2. In your opinion, the Chinese girl's action is one kind of contribution, or just a choice?

3. How do you think about the American husband's opinion that everyone should be responsible for his or her choice?

3. Parents and children

In China, parents are in power and they prefer coercion policy. Children are the center of a family, not only by the love of parents, but also by the love of grandparents. Chinese parents can play a major role in children's learning, work and marriage, ignoring their own idea and design of their life.

In America, parents are more democratic and progressive. They respect children's willing. Parents train their children to be independent from very young time. Children usually sleep alone when they left their babyhood. The family education prefers practice. Children earn money by helping parent do housework.

Questions

1. American children voluntarily move out of the family before marriage.
2. Chinese may think that they do not care about their families.
3. Children are likely expected to pay back the money loaned by their parents for their university education.
4. Many Chinese may think this displays lack of love and family feeling.
5. Parents emphasize fostering independence from an early age.
6. Chinese parents would think they fail to fulfill the most basic of parental responsibility.

5.3 Friendship

All people need friendship in their lives, which is established in different interactions with others, in offices, in schools, on social occasions, and so on. Generally speaking, among various cultures, there are both similarities and differences in how people make friends, how the circles of friends are formed, and what friends can talk about with one another.

5.3.1 Lead-in Cases

Case one

Chou was puzzled by Edward's reaction and felt a little hurt. He thought Edward did not take him as a real friend. They had known each other for two years since they shared the same apartment. Chou thought they had become good friends and could talk everything. But when he asked Edward about his job and the salary, Edward did not answer but changed the topic to the football match. Chou could not understand. He had told Edward everything. Why was Edward so indifferent?

Questions

1. Why did Edward refuse to answer Chou's question?
2. What should Chou do in this situation?

Case two

Yang Ruifang worked as a secretary in an Australian company in Melbourne. She became friendly with one of the Australian secretaries, a woman named Cathy Lane. The two usually ate lunch together and Yang Ruifang often asked Cathy for advice on problems she faced adjusting to Australian society. Cathy gave her a lot of advice and helped her move from one apartment to another. Cathy went with Yang Ruifang to the Immigration Bureau several times to help sort out some problems. Yang Ruifang visited Cathy several times at home but did not invite Cathy to her apartment because she shared it with four other people. If they did not see each other over the weekend, they usually talked on the telephone. As Yang Ruifang was also preparing to take an English test, she was able to get a lot of help with English in this way.

However, something seemed to be going wrong. Cathy seemed to be getting impatient, even a little cold. She started going out by herself at lunchtime instead of eating with Yang, and seemed reluctant to answer questions. Yang Ruifang was puzzled. She couldn't imagine what the problem was.

Questions

1. Why did Yang Ruifang think the relationship was developing well?
2. From this case what do you think Australians and other Westerners expect from their friends?
3. Give advice to Cathy and to Yang Ruifang to help them restore their friendship.

Case three

Are you short? Tall? Do you like pumpkins but hate mayonnaise? Whatever your interests, there's a club, society, or group for them.

America is home to about 25,000 clubs, associations, federations, societies, fraternal organizations, and other groups that all sorts of people join. If you are very short, there are

Interpersonal Relationships — Chapter Five

the "Short Stature Foundation" and the "Little People of America." If you're tall, there are dozens of clubs of tall people.

If you can't stand mayo, there's the "I Hate Mayonnaise" club; members get the No-mayo newsletter, and a list of mayo-free restaurants.

Many people claim to have seen the rock star Elvis Presley, even after his death in 1977. Maybe that's because so many people dress up and act like Elvis. Some of them formed the "Elvis Presley Impersonators Association International."

If you like to sing along through a microphone as you listen to music, you might consider the "Karaoke International Sing-Along Association".

The "International Organization of Nerds" has more than 10,000 members. It is led by a man in Cincinnati, Ohio, who calls himself the Supreme Archnerd. He says membership may be for you if your eyeglasses are held together with tape, you keep at least 37 ball-point pens in a plastic pocket protector, and you wear slacks and shirts of clashing plaids.

Many clubs are devoted to food. The "International Banana Club" wants people everywhere to smile more in a word that is "going bananas"(变得野蛮或疯狂). The club has a library and museum of about 12,000 important banana artifacts. The "international Pumpkin Association" is devoted to growing giant pumpkins. "Slow Food Foundation" is a club that objects to fast-food places and promotes the joy of leisurely dining.

Because so many people love animals, there are many clubs to protect favored creatures. For instance, "Bat Conservation International" wants people to know about the many good points of bats. One example: Bats eat tons of insects, which would otherwise bug people.

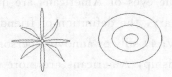

Questions

1. Why do you think there are so many clubs in the United States? Is this a way of making friends?
2. Are there so many clubs in China? Why or why not?
3. How do Chinese people make friends?

Case four

Now study the two graphs below. One represents the type of friends of a Chinese, and the other, that of an American. Discuss in small groups which is which. What differences are there between the two types of friends? Try to explain why.

Case five

Xiao Li is a Chinese student. One day her friend Linlin asked her to go shopping together. She was busy and really had no time to do that but she kept silent, put aside her work and went shopping with Linlin. Would you do the same as Xiao Li did? Do you think an American would do the same in similar situations? Why or why not?

Sometimes when you arrive in the States and ring your friend from the airport, he may tell you on the phone, "Take a 106 from the terminal", or "Get a taxi. Mind you get here in time for dinner".

Questions

1. How would you think of Xiao Li's decision?
2. How would you think of the American friend? Would you think he was giving you a cold welcome?

5.3.2 Friendly ≠ Friend ≠ Friendship

Westerners, in general, are friendly in communication. They use polite terms whenever they talk, to their family members, friends, and even strangers. "I'm sorry", "thank you" "please", etc., are all commonly heard expressions. However, their friendliness does not necessarily equal to the connotation of friendship which, in Chinese culture, indicates a life-long relationship with sincere dedication. Even the closest American friends still keep a certain distance in private lives due to the following reasons: First, the U.S. is a quite changing country, with the largest number of immigrants. Americans are used to moving their living places from here to there; second, the cultural value of individualism determines their way of living and treating people with a certain distance. Different from Chinese value that people should rely on friends when they are away from home, Americans believe in the principle of "give and take" as a basic criterion of choosing friends. This major difference in the value of friendship may sometimes leads to many misunderstandings or even conflicts in intercultural communications.

Although Chinese are more gentle and modest in character, in their heart the definition of friend and friendship is quite clear. Chinese are very serious in choosing friends. Chinese people make friends with like-minded people who share the similar interests, similar personalities, otherwise they cannot be real friends and they can only be regarded as ordinary.

Friends and friendship in the eyes of Americans are quite different from the Chinese people. In the American dictionary, the definition of friends varies widely: 1) person you like; 2) supporter; 3) not enemy; 4) silly or annoying person. The people to meet by chance can be friends. Thus, for friendship, Americans are more open and casual compared with Chinese.

5.3.3 Friendship Obligations

Friendship in Different Cultures
Linell Davis

In writing assignments in English classes my students frequently raise the topic of friendship. Reading what they write, I start to understand Chinese friendship obligations. For instance, once a student wrote that she understood that her friend wanted to go shopping. My student was busy and really had no time to do that, but she kept silent, put her work aside and went shopping with her friend; sometimes they write about middle school friends and describe the closeness they feel when they are together. Sometimes they write with great sadness when they feel they are no longer close to someone they considered a friend. All this is quite different from what American young people would say about friendship.

In the United States you can certainly ask a friend to do something with you, but you would not expect a friend to recognize and respond to your wishes without stating them. Nor would you expect a friend to drop everything to respond to a non-urgent need such as going shopping. In fact an American friend would feel that they had imposed too much if the friend gave up a real need to study to go shopping. There are limits to what you can expect from a friend. In the U. S. you feel free to ask your friend for help, but you recognize that the friend may say no, if they give you a reason. A friend in China is someone who, sensing that you are in need in some way, offers to assist you without waiting to be asked. In China there are few limits on what you can ask or expect of a friend. You can feel free to tell your friend what he or she can or should do to help you or please you.

Chinese expect friendships to be more lasting

Another difference is that my Chinese students seem to expect their friendships to stay the same over a long period of time maybe for a lifetime. A true friendship is a relationship that endures through changes in the lives of the friends. In the United States a person is likely to change even "best friends" several times over the years. Even this relationship in which people feel close emotionally and tell each other their secrets and personal problems may not survive life changes such as move to another city, graduation from a university, a significant change in economic circumstances, or the marriage of one of the friends. I think the reason is that friendship, like so many other relationships in the United States including marriage, depends on frequent interaction with the other person. If the people involved do not see each other and interact regularly, the relationship is likely to wither and die.

In the West, people often have many friends at one time, but the friendships are usually tied to specific circumstances or activities. When a person changes circumstances and activities, he or she changes friends. A person may have work friends, leisure activity friends and neighborhood friends. Also two people who are friends usually have similar financial circumstances. This is because friendships in the West are based on equality.

Friends should exchange similar activities and give similar things to one another. If one can afford to treat the other to a meal at an expensive restaurant and the other does not have enough money to do the same, it will cause a problem in the relationship.

Americans expect friends to be independent

As with so many other things in the West, people prefer to be independent rather than dependent, so they do not feel comfortable in a relationship in which one person is giving more and the other person is dependent on what is being given. For Westerners friendship is mostly a matter of providing emotional support and spending time together. Chinese friends give each other much more concrete help and assistance than Western friends do. A Chinese friend will use personal connections to help a friend get something hard to obtain such as a job, an appointment with a good doctor, an easier path through an official procedure or an introduction to another person who might also be able to give concrete help. Chinese friends give each other money and might help each other out financially over a long period of time. This is rarely part of Western friendships, because it creates dependence of one person on the other and it goes against the principle of equality.

American friends like Chinese friends give each other emotional support in times of trouble, but they do it differently. A Westerner will respond to a friend's trouble by asking, "What do you want to do?" The idea is to help the friend think out the problem and discover the solution he or she really prefers and then to support that solution. A Chinese friend is more likely to give specific advice to a friend. For instance, if in a friendship between two Chinese women, one woman is arguing with her husband, the friend might advise and she says so directly. An American friend in a similar situation may want her friend to choose wise actions too, but she will be very cautious about giving direct advice. Instead she may raise questions to encourage her friend to consider carefully what may happen if she does one thing instead of another.

Chinese can usually expect more from their friends than Americans can

Chinese people often communicate indirectly while Westerners tend to be more direct. In close personal relationships as friendship, the opposite is often the case. Talk between Chinese friends would probably sound too direct to Western ears. As we have seen Chinese codes of etiquette require more formal and polite interactions with strangers or guests than is typical in the West, but in China relationships with friends are much more informal than similar Western relationships.

Americans apologize to their friends for minor inconveniences such as telephoning late at night or asking for dome specific help. Even in close friendships Americans use polite forms such as "could you..." and "would you mind..." Because Chinese do not use these polite forms in their close relationships, and they probably do not use them when speaking English with Westerners they know well. As a result they may seem to be too direct or demanding to their Western friends. At the same time a Chinese person who is a friend of an American may be confused when the American continues to be formally polite after two have established their relationship.

Friends

Questions

1. What does friendship imply in Chinese culture?
2. What does friendship imply in American culture?
3. Summarize the major differences in people's attitudes towards friendship?

5.3.4 Extended Reading on Personal Network

Personal Network

Throughout much of Chinese history, the fundamental glue that has held society together is the concept of guanxi (关系), or relationships between people. It has been and remains a deep seated concept that lies at the core of Chinese society. It is very important for the Chinese to have good relationships. They often regard good social relations as a symbol of personal ability and influence. Someone who has no connections would be despised and is only half-Chinese. An established network of quality contacts can help accomplish almost anything, and thus having good relationships is a very powerful asset.

In China, there is another important vehicle in social exchange, that is, renqing (人情), which is literally translated as human sentiment or human emotion. A Western scholar once defines it as "covers not only sentiment but also its social expressions such as the offering of congratulations, or condolences or the making of gifts on appropriate occasions". In fact, renqing(人情) follows Confucian notion of reciprocity.

Such situation can also be found in Britain. Britain is society in which social class is still very important. In Britain, the accent people speak with, the clothes people wear, and the schools children attend are all markers that identify their social class. The education opportunity plays an important part in children's future lift, thus the school tie has been a clear marker of social class. If a child goes to a famous public school or well-known university, he will have more chances to know some "useful" persons who would give help in his future life. In Britain, there is a group of people called "the old boys' network", which means the group of men who went to school and university together. Such group of people not only dominates government, but also is very influential in banking, the media, the arts and education.

5.4 I/C Theory

5.4.1 Individualism & Individualist

Individualism refers to the habit or principle of being independent and self-reliant, or a social theory favoring freedom of action for individuals over collective or state control. In some countries, people are most likely to value individual identity, which means the social unit is the individual and the interests of the individual are considered to be more important than those of the group. These countries are individualist cultures, and can also be described as "I" cultures.

Individualists prefer to compete and negotiate openly. In an individualist group, members will say things like: "I don't agree with you"; "It won't work"; "What we need to do is ..." or "Your analysis doesn't go far enough." Such comments are said politely most of the time, but the words carry messages of disagreement or even conflict.

5.4.2 Collectivism & Collectivist

Collectivism refers to the practice or principle of giving a group priority over each individual in it. In other countries, people tend to place high value on group identity rather than individual identity, which means quite contrary to the individualist cultures, the interests of the individual are less important than those of the group. The social unit is the group. These countries are collectivist cultures, and can also be described as "We" cultures.

The disadvantage of collectivism is that the conflict is usually disguised and often occurs behind the scenes. This can make it more difficult to resolve. Collectivists, including Chinese, sometimes compete with others by creating problems for rivals rather than by trying to outperform them. This strategy maintains a harmonious surface for group life but often inhibits the initiative of group members. Over time it can drain off the energy of the group.

5.4.3 Attitudes and Behaviors between Individualists and Collectivists

Attitudes & Behaviors	Individualists	Collectivists
Self	Each person is separate from others; children learn to think in terms of "I"	Each person is part of a group; children learn to think in terms of "we"
Identity	Identity is based in the individual	Identity is based in the social network

Interpersonal Relationships — Chapter Five

continued

Attitudes & Behaviors	Individualists	Collectivists
Communication	Low context; speak your mind and tell the truth	High context; maintain harmony and avoid confrontations
Social Values	Personal freedom is more important than equality	Equality is more important than personal freedom
Decision-making	Follow universal rules; the decision-making process is important	Fulfill obligations to in-group relationships are important
Conformity	Group has relatively little influence on the behavior of group members	Group greatly influences the behavior of members
Cooperation	Cooperate with people who are not members of one's group plus group members	Cooperate with members of in-groups but not with members of out-groups
Self-reliance	It is a pleasure to do as much by yourself as possible	People depend on each other but should not burden in-group members unnecessarily
Typical Relationship Pattern	Short-term; voluntary less intensive relationships	Long-term; involuntary more intensive relationships

5.5 Review Tasks

I. Decide whether the following statements are true (T) or false (F).

1. To learn how to communicate in feminine or masculine style would help us win in the debate of the cross-gender communication. ( )

2. When you are confused in cross-gender communication, do not tend to make any judgment, otherwise the misunderstanding would occur possibly. ( )

3. The successful cross-gender communication depends on the validity of different communication styles. ( )

4. It is possible for men and women to apply a common rule in communication, even though they tend to apply different ones when interacting. ( )

5. In cross-gender communication, conversers could offer and also seek cues in trying to understand each other's meaning. ( )

6. Women can learn from masculine communication style how to support others. ( )

7. For individualists, equality is more important than personal freedom. ( )

8. To evaluate our positions and resist others' or otherwise would be an easy way to

make judgment in communication. ( )

9. The first and last principle for effective cross-gender communication is suspending judgment. ( )

10. Collectivist communication can be described as low context. ( )

11. Women are generally comfortable with building close relationships and confiding to others, while most men are reserved about involvement and disclosure. ( )

12. Most men use communication to create connection or equality between people. ( )

13. Family is the primary caretaker of a culture's core values and worldview and transmits them to new members of the culture. ( )

14. Generally speaking, in Western culture, it would be natural for family members to praise each other. ( )

15. Generally speaking, American children are more independent than Chinese children. ( )

16. It is impossible for a Chinese and an American to be true friends because they hold different views towards friendship. ( )

17. In countries with strong individualist features, people tend to place high value on group identity rather than individual identity. ( )

18. In China, friendship means a strong life-long bond between two people. ( )

19. American children have to remember too much knowledge by heart in primary school. ( )

20. In American, older parents usually live with their children, taking care of their grandchildren. ( )

Ⅱ. **Discuss the following questions.**

1. What are the characteristics of feminine talk and masculine talk respectively?

2. Are there any changes in the Chinese family structure now? If yes, what are the changes?

3. What are the differences in the concepts of friends between the Chinese and American cultures?

Ⅲ. **Analyze the following cases and answer the questions.**

Case one

Tom (Australian) and Lili (Chinese) are preparing to get married. Before being officially married, they sign a pre-nuptial agreement regarding their separate property. The assumption Tom holds is that as an individual each of them should protect their own rights and property in the event of a future divorce. Tom has had a bad experience from a legal perspective where his divorce made him quite poor when his ex-wife whom he loved for 20 years left him. What is different here is that he states this openly to his would-be wife. This kind of talk gives the Chinese woman the impression of preparing for a divorce instead of marriage, as they seem to be dividing property, making it very clear what is yours and what is mine.

In his talk about the agreement, Tom says that with the agreement when Lili dies, he could claim her property if she did not bestow it to others in the form of a will, and vice versa. He talks about death as naturally as about shopping. This is unacceptable in China. Such an agreement does focus attention on the motives and trust between people. It seems that Westerners are more materialistic, not bothering about any bad luck that might be brought about by mentioning something unwelcome.

Questions

1. Have you ever thought of signing an agreement before marriage (pre-nuptial agreement on separate property)?

2. Can you try to analyze why they each believe their ideas on the agreement is more reasonable?

Case two

Family structure and their inherent relationships and obligations are a major source of cultural difference.

The family is the center of most traditional Asian's lives. Many people worry about their families' welfare, reputation and honor. Asian families are often extended, including several generations related by blood or marriage living in the same home. An Asian person's misdeeds are not blamed just on the individual but also on the family—including the dead ancestors.

Traditional Chinese, among many other Asians, respect their elders and feel a deep sense of duty towards them. Children repay their parents' sacrifices by being successful and supporting them in old age. This is accepted as a natural part of life in China. In contrast, taking care of aged parents is often viewed as a tremendous burden in the United States, where aging and family support are not honored highly.

Filipinos, the most Americanized of the Asians, are still extremely family-oriented. They are dedicated to helping their children and will sacrifice greatly for their children to get an education. In turn, the children are devoted to their parents, who often live nearby. Grown children who go away and leave the country for economic reasons typically send large parts of their salary home to their parents and the rest of the family.

The Vietnamese family consists of people currently alive as well as the spirits of the dead and of the as-yet unborn. Any decisions or actions are done for family considerations, not individual desires. People's behavior is judged on whether it brings shame or pride to the family. Vietnamese children are trained to rely on their families, to honor elderly people, and to fear foreigners. Many Vietnamese think that their actions in this life will influence their status in the next life.

Fathers in traditional Japanese families are typical stern and aloof. Japanese college students in one study said that they would tell their fathers just about as much as they would tell a total stranger. The emotional and communication barrier between children and fathers in Japan appears very strong after children have reached a certain age.

Traditional Latin Americans are as family-centered as the traditional Asians. The family is the number one priority, the major frame of reference. Latin Americans believe that family members must help each other. Children in Latin America are taught to respect authority and are given many responsibilities at home. The Latin American family emphasizes authority with the males and older people being the most important. The family in most parts of Latin America includes many relatives, who remain in close contact. Family connections are the main way to get things done; dropping names (mentioning the names of important people the family knows) is often necessary to accomplish even simple things.

Although there has been much talk about "family values" in the United States, the family is not a usual frame of reference for decisions in the US mainstream culture. Family connections are not so important to most people. Dropping the names of wealthy or famous people the family knows is done in the United States, but it is not viewed positively. More important is a person's own individual "track record" of personal achievement.

Thus, many cultural differences exist in family structures and values. In some cultures, the family is the center of life and the main frame of reference for decisions. In other cultures, the family's reputation and honor depend on each person's actions: in other words, individuals can act without permanently affecting the family life. Some cultures values old people, while other cultures look down on them.

Questions

1. What cultural values can be found behind the family structures?
2. Is there anything in common in the values behind Asian family relationship?
3. Do you think there are some changes in the Chinese family structure? How do you account for them, if there are any?

IV. Extended Reading.

Gender and Friendship

Gender influences our friendships and has received much attention, as people try to figure out how different men and women's friendships are. There is a conception that men's friendships are less intimate than women's based on the stereotype that men do not express emotions. In fact, men report a similar amount of intimacy in their friendships as women but are less likely than women to explicitly express affection verbally (e. g., saying "I love you") and nonverbally (e. g., through touching or embracing) toward their same-gender friends. This is not surprising, given the societal taboos against same-gender expressions of affection, especially between men, even though an increasing number of men are more comfortable expressing affection toward other men and women. However, researchers have wondered if men communicate affection in more implicit ways that are still understood by the other friend. Men may use shared activities as a way to express closeness—for example, by doing favors for each other, engaging in friendly competition, joking, sharing resources, or teaching each other new skills. Some scholars have argued that there is a bias toward viewing intimacy as feminine, which may have skewed research on men's friendships. While verbal expressions of intimacy through self-disclosure have been noted as important features of women's friendships, activity sharing has been the focus in men's friendships. This research doesn't argue that one gender's friendships are better than the other's, and it concludes that the differences shown in the research regarding expressions of intimacy are not large enough to impact the actual practice of friendships.

Cross-gender friendships are friendships between a male and a female. These friendships diminish in late childhood and early adolescence as boys and girls segregate into separate groups for many activities and socializing, reemerge as possibilities in late adolescence, and reach a peak potential in the college years of early adulthood. Later, adults with spouses or partners are less likely to have cross-sex friendships than single people. In any case, research studies have identified several positive outcomes of cross-gender friendships. Men and women report that they get a richer understanding of how the other gender thinks and feels. It seems these friendships fulfill interaction needs not as commonly met in same-gender friendships. For example, men reported more than women that they rely on their cross-gender friendships for emotional support. Similarly, women reported that they enjoyed the activity-oriented friendships they had with men.

As discussed earlier regarding friends-with-benefits relationships, sexual attraction presents a challenge in cross-gender heterosexual friendships. Even if the friendship does not include sexual feelings or actions, outsiders may view the relationship as sexual or even encourage the friends to become "more than friends". Aside from the pressures that come with sexual involvement or tension, the exaggerated perceptions of differences between men and women can hinder cross-gender friendships. However, if it were true that men and women are too different to understand each other or be friends, then how could any long-term partnership such as husband/wife, mother/son, father/daughter, or brother/sister be successful or enjoyable?

(https://en.wikipedia.org/wiki/Gender)

Questions

1. What is cross-gender friendship and when do people usually develop cross-gender friendship?

2. What are the possible advantages of developing cross-gender friendship?

Naming and Addressing

> "Careful with fire", is good advice, we know; "Careful with words", is ten times doubly so.
>
> —Will Carleton
>
> It's not what he said, but the way he said it.
>
> —English Proverb

6.1 Cultural Differences in Naming

Personal names are not only linguistic symbols that distinguish one person from others, but also social symbols, representing relationship in societies and cultures. Personal name is "a mirror of culture".

6.1.1 Origins of Chinese Family Names

It is thought that Chinese family names came about in matriarchal clan society. At that time, every clan got the distinctive clan name based on their totem or dwelling places. The clan names are the earliest family names which in Chinese are called 姓(xìng). After population of a clan (tribe) multiplied, the clan divided into several branches and moved to different places to live. Then each branch would get their own branch name to distinguish this branch from the others. The name of each branch is called 氏(shì). "Xìng" is not changeable, but "shì" can be changed.

In Xia, Shang and Zhou Dynasties, "xìng" and "shì" began to have class color besides their original function. "Shì", especially, was best owned by their ruler. As a result, "shì" became the mark of the aristocracy. Only the aristocrats had "shì", and the ordinary people had no "shì". All the aristocrats were men at that time. Therefore, only men had "shì". The distinction between "xìng" and "shì" disappeared in Qin and Han Dynasty. They became one that is called "xìngshì" in Chinese and refers to family names.

  Chinese names can give all sorts of information about a person. Some names tell us something about parents' expectation for the children, values, personal characteristics or gender. Some of Chinese surnames may come from the names of ancient kingdoms or areas, from ancestor's names, from official titles or historical events, and some indicate family relationships. Nowadays the origins of surnames are often neglected and people pay much attention to the meanings of their given names.

  Examples of male names and female names:

王刚—strong and firm

张海—big and broad-minded

赵雅芳—elegant and fragrant, pleasant and graceful

李淑贤—kind, gentle and virtuous

In Chinese, male names tend to connote firmness, strength, the power and grandeur of nature, moral values, etc., whereas female names often suggest elegance, manners, virtues, the beauty of nature.

6.1.2　Origins of English Names

  Several hundred years ago in England there were only first names. Surnames were gradually introduced as a way of distinguishing between people who had the same given name.

  English family names are the historical product of English society. They experienced nearly three centuries from nonexistence to full development. There was a time when no one had a hereditary family name. "When the ancestors of English people invaded Britain in the 5th century, they formed a tribal society. English people didn't get family names until 1066 when Normans conquered Britain. The Normans certainly didn't have a fully developed family names system." It was not yet their conscious policy to identify a family by one name. But there were not enough names for distinction. In a certain period, more and more names were duplicated. This phenomenon brought great trouble to people in communication. So when people were talking about a person who was absent, they often employed additional phrases for further identification. For example, when they referred to John who lived under the hill, they would add descriptive phrase as "from the hill". Then John became "John from the hill" to indicate which John they were talking about.

  Although the additional phrases can play the role for further identification, they are too complicated. Therefore, some unimportant words are often omitted. Then "John from the hill" is changed into "John Hill". With the development of feudal society, there was an urgent need for people to solve the problem of personal identification. For this reason, people created a new way for expression that they began to add their father's or manor's name behind their given name. In fact, the additional phrases which are called "bynames(别名,绰号)" are the beginning stage of English family names. They played an important transitional part in the development of English family names. Gradually, these bynames were turned into hereditary family names.

English family names were drawn from a number of sources: 1) Place of identity: Some names indicate where the person came from, e.g., Norman, Moor, Hall, Chesterfield, and Wood, Brooks, Hill, York, du Nord（来自北方）, von Bayern（巴伐利亚人）, Ashby（紧靠岑树的房子） and Byfield（紧靠田野）; 2) Occupation: These names are picked to indicate the occupations, as Clark, Cook, Taylor, Carter, Smith, Chapman, Cooper, Abbot, Baker, Turner, Butler, Thatcher, Chandler, Shumacher and Giardino; 3) Family relationships & ethnic identities: Surnames were also coined from first names to indicate family relationships and ethnic sources as well, with suffix "-s", "-son", "-kins" and prefix "M-", "Mc-", "Mac-", "Fitz" such as Robertson, Donaldson, Watkins, Thomas in England; MacDonald in Scotland; O'Patrick in Ireland; and in Norway, Larsson ("for the son of Lar"), Haraldsdottir (the daughter of Harald); 4) Personal characteristic: There are also many English names used to show personal characteristics, such as Young, Longfellow, Wisdom, Moody, Rich, Fox, Newman (a newcomer to the area), Little, Sharpe, Brown, White, Short.

In America, female names also connote gentler qualities by referring to flower, birds and those feeble creatures and etc. Male names are usually concerned with God/Lord and religion, so are some female names.

Examples of male names:
Adam 亚当, 希伯来文, 天下第一个男人
Mike 麦克, 像上帝的人
Samuel 被上帝听到的人
Examples of female names:
Rose（玫瑰）, Daisy（雏菊）, Jasmine（茉莉花）,
Lily（百合花）, Yolanda（紫罗兰）, Melissa（蜜蜂）.

6.2　Number of Syllables of First Names

Female names tend to be longer with more syllables, such as trisyllabic.
　e.g.: Katherine（凯瑟琳）, Elizabeth（伊丽莎白）, Amanda（阿曼达）, Victoria（维多利亚）…
Male names tend to be much more monosyllabic (one-syllabic) and short.
　e.g.: Jim（吉姆）, John（约翰）, Bob（鲍勃）, Joe（乔）…

6.3　Last Sound of First Names

Female names more likely end in a vowel, e.g. Linda（琳达）, Tracy（特蕾西）, Patricia（帕特里夏）, Deborah（黛博拉）, and Barbara（芭芭拉）; or very likely end in a nasal as in

107

Jean（珍）, Kathleen（卡斯琳）, Sharon（莎伦）, Ann（安）.

Male names much more likely end in a plosive (consonant), e.g. Bob（鲍勃）, David（大卫）, Dick（迪克）, and Jack（杰克）.

6.4 Further Reading

We all know that names have meanings. For example, Chinese names can give all sorts of information about a person. They may give clues about where and when the person was born. Or they may tell us something about family relationships, ethnic group, parents' expectation for the children, sex (though nowadays it is more difficult to tell a girl's name from a boy's), values or even personal characteristics. However, naming is different in other cultures, and so it takes effort to understand the implication of foreign and the rules governing their use.

A common practice among students in China who learn a foreign language is to have a name in the target language. When we do so, we need to be careful about the meanings of foreign names. The following passage by Ann Aungles may help bear out this point.

When my mother was a young girl, her father was killed in a work accident on the London Docks. Her mother, unable to care for five children, sent three of them, my mother and a younger brother and sister to be looked after in an orphanage in 1910.

At that time orphanage in England had two functions: to care for the children and to fill the constant demand for trained domestic servants. In 1916, my mother, 14, became a housemaid in a castle in Scotland. The lady of the house instructed the housekeeper that this new maid was to be known as "Florrie" instead of her own name "Florence".

It was the standard of the day. The upper classes regularly renamed their servants to fit their "servant class" which were lesser beings in the household.

Renaming, of course, was also a feature of slavery and servitude in Australia and the USA. Today Afro-American and indigenous Australian historians record this enforced cultural dispossession of their grand parents and great grandparents as a significant aspect of the gross racism of that era.

So it is a shock to some visiting lecturers in Beijing that students are willing to adopt English names. Names are loaded with symbolism, sometimes positive, sometimes negative. Yet the connotations attached to any one name may not be clear unless one has lived in that country from which it has been derived. But how are students to know the subtleties of naming without fully participating in the life and culture that create these complex layers of meaning.

The results can be disturbing. There is an unease in speaking with a sophisticated, wise, mature young person whose name would be used only by children in England or America. In addition, Western societies are notorious for their consumerism. They are societies of instant disposability. In some ways names are like clothes. Out-of-date names can be an awful embarrassment to young adults.

I am glad that I do not have to take on a name whose cultural underpinnings are a mystery to me. However, it would be good to know what students feel about their English names. Is renaming a pleasure or inconvenience? Does it instill a sense of alienation and cultural aspect of being an English learner in China?

Question

Do you have an English name and why do you choose it as yours?

6.5 Cultural Differences in Forms of Address

6.5.1 Case Discussion

Case one

Linda White taught English at a primary school in China. This is her first time to live in China. When she came into her office for the first time, she introduced herself, "My name is Linda White. If you like, you can call me 'Linda'." Then one of her new colleagues introduced himself, "My name is Zhou Yang (周洋). Call me Zhou Yang." Linda looked confused. She didn't knew which one the family name was, "Zhou" or "Yang", and she didn't know why she should use the whole name to call her new colleague.

Questions

1. Why did Linda feel confused?
2. What can account for Linda's bewilderment?
3. How should Zhou Yang introduce himself to Linda?

Case two

It was the first day that Linda White had her English class. At her class, she told her students, "My name is Linda White. If you like, you can call me 'Linda'. Now I'd like you to tell me your names. Let's start with you." Then the first student answered, "Yes, Teacher. Let me introduce myself. My name is Zhang Nancy."

Linda told her student, "Well, please don't call me 'Teacher'. You can use 'Linda' or

'Ms. White'." The student looked confused.

Questions

1. Why did Linda White ask her students call her "Linda" or "Ms. White", but not "Teacher"?
2. Why did Zhang Nancy look confused?

6.5.2 Ways of Addressing

Address form is one of markers of politeness and is an indispensable part of communication. An appropriate address form promotes interpersonal communication smoothly. An address form is polite in one culture, but might be inappropriate in another culture. Address forms reflect the features of a language culture. People from different countries and cultures have specific ways of addressing and greeting others when making new acquaintances. Not knowing how to address someone properly can be a very embarrassing situation for both parties. Generally speaking, English address forms are less complicated than Chinese address terms. For instance, we cannot translate Chinese forms *Xiao Li* and *Lao Zhang* literally into "Little Brown" and "Old Jones".

In recent years, the trend of many English-speaking people has been to address others by using the first name—Tom, Michael, Linda, Jane, etc. rather than calling the person Mr. Summers, Mrs. Howard or Miss Jones. This is especially common among Americans, even when people meet for the first time. This applies not only to people of roughly the same age, but also of different ages. It is not a sign of discreet. It is not at all uncommon to hear a child calling a much older person—Joe, Ben, May, Helen, etc. This may even include the child's parents or grandparents. People of different social status do the same. For example, many college students call their professors by their first names. The professors do not regard this as a sign of disrespect or familiarity, but rather, as an indication that the professor is affable and has a sense of equality. This, of course, is quite opposite to Chinese custom. One can imagine the reactions of adults if a child were to call a grandparent by his or her first name, or a student did the same in calling a teacher, which will be considered impolite in Chinese culture.

In China, we usually address a stranger, even an acquaintance, with some titles, such as "大爷"(grandpa), "大妈"(grandma), "大叔"(uncle), "大婶"(aunty). The extension of kinship terms is a feature of Chinese culture. Terms such as "uncle, aunt, grandpa, granny, sister and brother" are used as honorific titles for senior people or strangers. Native speakers of English would be puzzled if they are addressed in this way by people outside the immediate family. Literary translation of those terms may sound odd to English-speaking people. Even with relatives, English-speaking people tend to only use the first name and leave out the terms of relationship.

Some people may say that there is Brother Joseph or Sister Mary in English; however, these terms would commonly be understood as religious or professional society. In America, people usually use "Hi", or "Could you tell me...?" to address a stranger. And if there is a difference in status or age between two individuals, formal titles and last names are used unless the person of lower status is told to use the first name. For example:

Accountant (age 50): Hello, my name is Bob Thomas.

Clerk (age 20): It's nice to meet you, Mr. Thomas.

Accountant: just call me Bob, Please.

And also the kinship terms for both the paternal and maternal sides in Chinese culture are different. However, the English kinship terms, such as uncle, cousin, aunt, grandpa and grandma have no difference between paternal and maternal sides, as shown in the following examples:

Chinese terms	English terms
奶奶、姥姥	grandma
爷爷、外公	grandpa
公公、岳父	father-in-law
婆婆、岳母	mother-in-law
伯父、叔叔、舅舅	uncle
姑妈、姨妈、伯母、舅妈	aunt
堂兄弟（姊妹）、表兄弟（姊妹）	cousin
小叔子、小舅子	brother-in-law
小姑子、小姨子	sister-in-law
侄儿、外甥	nephew
侄女、外甥女	niece

In Chinese, address forms are oriented by generation, age, paternal and maternal relationship and in-law relationship. In a Chinese family, a younger child should address the elder as elder brother (哥哥) or elder sister (姐姐) instead of names in English culture, otherwise, a younger child addressing old sisters' or brothers' names will be considered impolite and might be punished or scolded. In English-speaking culture, sisters and brothers address each other's name. People address their neighbors, friends and colleagues by their names after the introduction was over.

It is also quite common for the Chinese to use position-linked or occupation-linked titles to address people, such as "王经理" (Manager Wang), "张主任" (Director Zhang), "马局

长" (Director General Ma). In more formal situations, the title along with the last name is appropriate.

Americans have only a limited number of titles to be used before a person's last name—Doctor, Professor, Judge, President, Senator, Governor, Mayor, General, Colonel, Captain, Father, etc. Terms like teacher, manger and director are occupations or positions. In English, only a few occupations or titles would be used: Doctor Smith is common for those who have qualified in the medical profession, and Judge Smith for those authorized to try cases in law courts; Governor Smith and Mayor Smith may be used for those who hold such offices, although often without the name. The same with Professor Smith. However, there are very few others.

As a result, no wonder Americans are surprised to see that it is important to clearly indicate their positions in their company at a business meeting, because Chinese always treat them differently according to their ranks and status.

English translations of Chinese literary works usually keep such forms as Grandpa, Auntie, Sister-in-law, but they sound strange to the English ear. In English-language writing about China, such terms are used in order to keep or give a Chinese flavor to the story. Some of these terms, though, are especially troublesome. How to address a teacher has long been a problem. Should it be Teacher or Teacher Zhang? Neither of these is keeping with the English custom. Should we say Comrade or Comrade Li, which is not widely accepted in non-socialist countries? Or should we simply follow the English custom and call the teacher Mr. Zhang, Mrs. Yang? All of these would sound terrible to Chinese if school-age youngsters were to do so.

Other different terms are "师傅","警察叔叔", and "解放军叔叔". If we translate the former one into "master", it would carry the meaning of a master-servant relationship. If we translate "警察叔叔" and "解放军叔叔" into "Uncle Policeman" and "Uncle P. L. A." respectively, they would sound very strange to the Westerners. There are two reasons. One reason is that many foreigners do not know, P. L. A. stands for "中国人民解放军"; the other reason is that the relationship between policeman, P. L. A. and people is closer in China than that in Western countries. The Westerners do not know why people call them uncles.

Interestingly, there is no general term in English for getting the attention of a stranger, or of a person whose name we may not know. In Chinese we have "同志", or "师傅", and now the fashionable "小姐" or "先生", but what do people do in English if such a need arises? Depending on the situation, English customs might suggest using such expressions as "Excuse me", "Pardon me", or in England, "I say here". Expressions like "Hey", or "Hey you" or "You", are used, but are not considered polite. Often, people resort to a way that needs no language. They simply clear their throat loudly, or make some noise or gesture to attract the person's attention.

Naming and Addressing

Chapter Six

Questions

1. Summarize the general rules of addressing people in the Western culture.
2. Summarize the general rule of addressing people in Chinese culture.
3. Compare the two address forms above mentioned and find out the major differences, and add some more examples.
4. What have you learned about the proper way of addressing in different cultures? Use your personal experience to explain.

6.5.3 Case Discussion

Case one

An American tourist is traveling by train in China. Sitting opposite to him is a Chinese passenger. They introduce themselves to each other...

American tourist: Hello, I'm Adam O'Patrick. Glad to meet you.

Chinese passenger: Hello, my name is Wang Lin. I'm glad to meet you, too. Where do you come from, Mr. Adam?

American tourist: I'm from America. Please just call me Adam, Mr. Lin.

Chinese passenger: And you may just call me Wang Lin.

Question

Is there something wrong as to the ways of addressing in the above case?

Case two

A British tourist is visiting a Chinese family. The Chinese hostess introduces herself and her husband to the guest...

Chinese hostess: Welcome to my home. My name is Li Hong, and this is my husband.

British tourist: Thank you, Mrs. Li. It's a pleasure to meet you. Mr. Li. I'm Anna Thatcher.

Chinese hostess: Have a seat, Madam Anna.

Question

Is there anything wrong as to the ways of addressing in the above case?

Case three

An American visiting scholar called Prof. Robert Johnson is now teaching in Zhejiang University. His wife Rebecca and six-year-old son David have been living with him in Hangzhou for one year. David learns Chinese in the attached kindergarten of Zhejiang University. Chen Yilian is a Chinese student of Prof. Johnson.

One weekend she came to visit them; his wife was just out for a moment. Below is their conversation.

Prof. Johnson: Hello, Chen, come in please! How are you?

Chen Yilian: I'm fine, thank you. And you, Prof. Johnson?

Prof. Johnson: Fine too, thanks. Just call me Robert. Dave, this is Chen Yilian from Zhejiang University. Say hello to her.

David: Hi, Yilian Ayi.

Chen Yilian to David: Well, you can speak very good Chinese. But just call me Chen Ayi.

Questions

1. Why does Prof. Johnson address Chen Yilian as Chen but asks her to address himself Robert?

2. Why does David address her as Yilian Ayi?

6.6 Kinship

6.6.1 Kin Terms in China

In China kin terms are not only used within one's own family but also to other people. The appropriate use of kin terms may reflect a person's politeness, respectfulness, and friendliness.

Whereas in China children address them with the title only, and the titles can tell whether they are from their father or mother's side and whether they are older or younger than their father or mother. The way of addressing them by their first names without adding a title couldn't be applied in Chinese families because it would be regarded as impolite and disrespectful.

6.6.2 Kin Terms in Britain

However, in Britain kin terms are mainly confined to family members, though some families still keep the tradition of having children use kin terms when addressing adults who are close neighbors and family friends.

In Britain children address their parents' brothers and sisters with the title of Uncle or Aunt plus their first names, or simply by their names without adding a title.

The kin terms do not distinguish between paternal and maternal relatives, nor between relatives according to birth order.

6.6.3 Case Discussion

Read the following cases and discuss the questions after each one.

(1) The young lady Marilyn, a major character in Family Album, USA, addresses her mother-in-law by her first name, Ellen. How do you account for this? Could the same thing happen in China? Why?

(2) In China we address a stranger with an advanced age "Grandpa" or "Grandma". Why do we do so since that stranger is not connected to us by blood? How does this sound to an English ear?

6.7 Review Tasks

Ⅰ. Decide whether the following statements are true (T) or false (F).

1. Many students call their professors by their given names in most English-speaking countries. ( )
2. We can address Roger Williams, who is an officer, as Officer Williams. ( )

3. Ranks in the armed forces like Captain, Mayor, General are often used as titles in English. ( )

4. In Chinese there are no differences between paternal and maternal kinship terms. ( )

5. Don't take offense—getting the form of address "wrong" is rarely intended to be offensive. ( )

6. Addressing forms like "Miss Mary", "Mr. Brown" by the Chinese may be a form of cultural compromise. ( )

7. Usually Westerners do not understand what "Uncle Policeman" or "P. L. A. Uncle" in Chinese means as a way of addressing. ( )

8. If Jason Douglas is a lawyer, we can call him Lawyer Douglas. ( )

9. The way of addressing Chinese people by their first names without adding a title would be regarded as polite and respectful. ( )

10. In English, the kin terms distinguish between paternal and maternal relatives, and also between relatives according to birth order. ( )

11. There is no general term in English for getting the attention of a stranger, or of a person whose name we may not know. ( )

12. Expressions like "Hey", or "Hey you" or "You", are used to draw the attention of a stranger in English and are considered polite. ( )

13. Americans often indicate their positions in their company at a business meeting, because they always treat them differently according to their ranks and status. ( )

14. In Chinese culture, surnames were gradually introduced as a way of distinguishing between people who had the same given name. ( )

15. It is uncommon for the Chinese to use position-linked or occupation-linked titles to address people. ( )

16. Today in China, people often address their neighbors, friends and colleagues by their names after the introduction was over, regardless of their age and occupations. ( )

17. In China, many people's names are concerned with religion and ethnic sources. ( )

18. English male names much more likely end in a vowel, while female names in a plosive (consonant). ( )

19. Both English and Chinese names could show personal characteristics. ( )

20. In English, male names tend to connote firmness, strength, the power and grandeur of nature, moral values, etc., whereas female names often suggest elegance, manners, virtues, the beauty of nature. ( )

Ⅱ. **Discuss the following questions.**

1. Do you have an English name? If yes, why? How did you choose it?

2. Discuss the differences in addressing people between English and Chinese cultures.

3. Suppose you are teaching an international freshman from your university the Chinese way of addressing, plan a short lesson with your group and share with the class.

III. **Analyze the following cases and answer the questions.**

Case one

Leanna Adams is an American who worked as a language teacher at a university in China. The following is describing her first English class with her Chinese students:

I told my students that they could call me Leanna. When I opened the floor for the students to ask me questions, there was complete silence. The students paired off then, whispering with each other and avoiding my eyes.

After a while, a girl stood up and asked "Teacher, my name is Gypsy. I want to know, why do you leave your boyfriend to come to China?" At that moment, I didn't feel too lonely, so I said, "I wanted to come see China. China is an economic super power and I love Chinese food." The class cheered. This was exactly what they wanted to hear. I didn't add that I came to China to get away from my job in a cubicle or that I needed a life change and didn't know where else to go.

Questions

1. What might cause the possible intercultural misunderstandings in this case?
2. Why do you think is the real reason for the American teacher to come to China?

Case two (continued)

"Teacher, my name is Tea because I come from a region known for its tea."
"Teacher, my name is Apple. I like playing balls, dancing, skating."
"Teacher, my name is Smile. I don't like sports. I like dancing."

I had no idea that they would name themselves after fruit, food, mannerisms and elves. While taking six years of now-forgotten French, I had never once considered naming myself Bicyclette (French, which means "bicycle") or Bleu (French, which means "blue"). Many of them said that their names in English sounded like their given Chinese names. Others told me that they chose the English meaning of their given names. Others, like Coca and Cola, were best friends.

Questions

1. What went wrong in students' self-introduction?
2. If you were the Chinese student, how are you going to explain the Chinese naming culture to your American teacher?

IV. **Extended Reading.**

How to Address a Stranger in Chinese

Introduction—亲 (qīn) vs. 亲爱的

If you've ever shopped on Taobao, a Chinese website that's kind of like Amazon or eBay, then you've probably been called "qīn(亲)" by a complete stranger before. Vendors on Taobao call buyers "qīn", which is actually a term of endearment. Calling someone "qīn" is like calling them "dear", and it's short for "qīn ài de(亲爱的)".

Let me explain why I think this is interesting. Actually, calling someone "qīn" is really just an abbreviated form of a standard polite letter salutation, as in "Qīn ài de [name], nín hǎo! (亲爱的 [name], 您好!)", which means "Dear [name], hello!" But the thing is, by shortening it to just "qīn", it becomes much more casual and much more personal, like something that would normally be used between people who are actually very familiar with and fond of each other.

Before I get into why I think complete strangers online use the word "qīn" with each other, let me give you another example of an odd word choice.

Addressing people by 美女 (měi nǚ) and 帅哥 (shuài gē)

One way that people in China often address women who they don't know is 美女 (měi nǚ), as in, "Hey, měi nǚ, is my grande caramel latte ready yet?" "Měi nǚ" means "beautiful woman" or "beautiful girl", so the first time someone called me 美女 (měi nǚ), I was so flattered. By calling me "měi nǚ" instead of "miss" or "madam", the shop assistant instantly created a connection between us and made me feel good. But the nice, flattered feeling only lasted for about 10 seconds, until I noticed that she was calling every female in the shop "měi nǚ". As I learned that day, any girl or woman can be called "měi nǚ" these days, and when used this way, calling someone "měi nǚ" isn't really a comment on her looks, despite the actual meaning of the word.

The same thing happens with males now too. Some people will call any random guy 帅哥 (shuài gē), which means "handsome man", with no regard for whether he is actually good-looking or not.

So why do people use these words? My guess is, if you're trying to sound casual, friendly, and approachable towards someone whose name you don't know, it's tough to come up with a better alternative. This is especially true if you're trying to create a personal connection with him or her. For example, I think 亲 (qīn) became the standard way for Taobao vendors to address customers because, compared to using other more traditional ways of addressing a customer, the term 亲 (qīn) is a clever way for the vendor to create a sense of closeness and familiarity with the buyer. Besides, it also keeps the mood of the conversation light and casual, which is important when the interactions are happening online and you can't rely on body language or tone of voice.

Even so, it is a bit strange to call just anyone "qīn" or "měi nǚ" or "shuài gē", and there are plenty of people in China who cringe a bit when they hear others use these words so liberally. Let's talk about the alternatives:

Alternative 1—小姐 (xiǎo jiě)

This term, which means "miss", is not only restricted by age, but can seem overly formal and can have some negative connotations. It's no longer really appropriate to use this term with a woman who has reached her thirties or so. It's commonly used with someone's last name, such as 王小姐（wáng xiǎo jiě）without any connotations, good or bad. But, when used on its own, it's often to either address someone formally or to call to women who work in the service industry, especially waitresses. And in some parts of China, "xiǎo jiě" is a term used to refer to a prostitute. So you can see why some people hesitate to use this word in some contexts.

Alternative 2—女士（nǚ shì）

This term means "madam" or "lady" and is generally used for women over 40 or so. It's very polite, and often too polite for many settings. Add that to the fact that it's only used for older ladies, and you've got plenty of room for the possibility of having an awkward interaction or even offending someone. It's just not a word that you want to use when you're trying to create a personal connection or keep the tone light.

Alternative 3—先生（xiān sheng）

This means "sir" or "mister". Just like the English equivalents, it can be used for males of all ages, married or unmarried, so there's no worry about offending someone in that way. But like 小姐（xiǎo jiě）and 女士（nǚ shì）, the word 先生（xiān sheng）is just a bit stiff and mostly used in a polite situation, so not the best choice for a more casual interaction.

Alternative 4—同志（tóng zhì）

Okay, this is not really a viable alternative. This means "comrade" and was commonly used in mainland China for a period, but hasn't been used anymore for years. Actually, it's now mostly used to refer to homosexuals. I only list this word here because, purely from a linguistic standpoint, I think it's a kind of a shame that 同志（tóng zhì）isn't used anymore. Back in the day, just about anyone could safely use it with anyone else, without any worry of offending someone.

As you can see, you're not left with many choices if you want to get someone's attention but don't know his/her name, and you don't want to just say "hey". So without many alternatives to choose from, people got creative and started using other words that originally had a different meaning or were used in different contexts.

Conclusion

Now, the final question is, should YOU start using words like 美女（měi nǚ）and 帅哥（shuài gē）to call out to strangers? That depends on the situation and the message that you are trying to convey. Do keep in mind that a girl calling a girl "美女（měi nǚ）" and a guy calling a girl "美女（měi nǚ）" can come across quite differently. The same goes for 帅哥（shuài gē）.

I don't know if anyone actually gets offended by being called 美女（měi nǚ）or 帅哥（shuài gē）, but I do know that some people still find these terms a bit awkward, even though they can't think of a better alternative.

As for me, maybe I'm just getting old, but personally, I rarely use these words. I generally find them to be a little too flirtatious for my style. The only time I might use these words is, for example, in a bar or some place like that with a very casual atmosphere, and I'd only use it to joke around with people who are quite young, say 25 or younger.

In the right setting, it can be a fun way to get a smile from someone who's not expecting to be called that by a foreigner. But if in doubt, and you just want to play it safe, you can always just say "你好（nǐ hǎo）" to get someone's attention.

If I were in the habit of using those words, I'd probably end this post by saying something like this: "So, how about all you 帅哥们（shuāi gē men）and 美女们（měi nǚ men）out there?" Would you ever call a complete stranger 帅哥（shuài gē）or 美女（měi nǚ）? And would you feel awkward or even offended if someone else called you that, or would it actually make you feel good?

(Adapted from http://www.yoyochinese.com/blog)

Questions

1. How would you answer the last question the author raises at the end of this article?

2. Besides the ways of addressing mentioned in this article, what are the other ways you could think of for addressing strangers in China?

3. Do a research with your group on "How to Address Stranger in French/English/Urdu/Japanese/Korean/...".

Chapter Seven
Culture-loaded Words in Communication

> *No one when he uses a word has in mind exactly the same thing that another has, and the differences, however tiny, sends its tremors throughout language.*
>
> —Wilhelm von Humboldt
>
> *The limits of my language are the limits of my world.*
>
> —Ludwig Wittgenstein

In the language system, culture-loaded words are the vocabulary which can best embody the cultural information that a language carries and they also reflect the social life.

In both English and Chinese, there are large numbers of culture-loaded words, which have their specific cultural connotation, such as "dragon" and "知识分子". Does "dragon" mean the same to a Westerner as "龙" to a Chinese? Does "知识分子" have the same meaning as its counterpart "intellectual"? The answer to these two questions would seem to be YES. The Chinese for "dragon" is "龙" in all the English-Chinese dictionaries; the same with "知识分子" for "intellectual". But there exist differences.

In Chinese culture, "龙" is a totem with many royal associations, such as "龙心大喜" "龙袍" "龙床". However, the associations of "dragon" to Westerners are horrible, disgusting monsters. Likewise, in China, the term "知识分子" generally refers to those who have received higher education including college teachers, college students, middle school teachers, and such people as medical doctors, engineers, interpreters, etc. However, in the U.S. and Europe, "intellectual" includes only people of high academic status such as college professors, not ordinary college students. So the term covers a much smaller range of people.

This chapter is mainly concerned with the connotative meanings of culture-loaded words reflected in colors, proverbs and idioms, numbers as well as taboo words.

7.1 Colors

7.1.1 Lead-in Case

Mr. Smith, a very white man, but a very yellow one. He was very red with anger when he found himself cheated by his close friend, but he said nothing. Last Friday, a black letter day, he had a car accident. He was looking rather green and feeling blue lately. When I saw him, he was in a brown study. I hope he'll soon be in the pink again.

Question

What do the colors mean?

7.1.2 Cultural Differences in Colors

1. White and Red

From cultural and anthropological standpoint, red in Chinese culture comes from the Sun, because the burning of light symbols luminosity(光明). Chinese ancestors sacrificing and worshiping to the Sun has an instinctive attachment to it. Red symbolizes good luck and happiness. For example:

- We call the person who lead others to a marriage "matchmaker"(红娘);
- We hang big red lantern in happy days, with red couplets(对联) and red characters;
- Men and women in wedding put big red "喜";
- The liveliness, prosperity is called "红火"; bustling, lively place "红尘".

Red also symbolizes revolution and progress, e. g. the Communist regime was originally called "红色政权". Red also symbolizes smoothness, success and benefits, e. g. a person who gets the boss's appreciation is called "红人". Red also symbolizes beauty, such as "红袖""红妆""红颜".

As to white, in the initial stages of human beings, our ancestors, the weak and the powerless, could not resist the fierce beasts attack. In the daytime they were fully exposed, and readily eaten by wild beasts. So they had instinctive fears to white. In this way, white in Chinese culture became a color taboo. 穿白衣,戴白帽,帖白纸,白事. Besides, "白" in Chinese indicates clearness, and effortlessness, such as 表白,真相大白,白费工夫. In translation, Chinese character "白" in fact has little to do with "white". For examples:

- "白开水" plain boiled water

Cultural-loaded Words in Communication

- "白字" wrongly written or mispronounced character
- "白搭" no use/ no good
- "白费事" all in vain, a waste of time and energy
- "白手起家" to build from nothing

In English culture, white symbolizes purity. For examples:

- a white soul 纯洁的心灵
- white wedding 新娘穿白色礼服的婚礼

It also symbolizes upright, honesty. For examples:

- a white spirit 正直的精神
- white men 高尚、有教养的人
- white hand 廉洁、诚实

And it symbolizes good luck. For examples:

- one of the white days in one's life 某人生活中的吉日之一
- white magic 有天使相助的

It also symbolizes ignorance and legal. For examples:

- white market 合法市场
- white list 经过批准的合法名单
- a white lie 无恶意的谎话

In English culture, red symbolizes brutality, bloodshed and being offensive in western culture. For examples:

- the red rules of tooth and claw 残杀和暴力统治
- a red battle 血战
- red hot political campaign 激烈的政治活动
- a red revolution 赤色革命
- red activities 左派激进活动

2. Yellow

In Chinese, yellow is the symbol of "honor", "dignity" and "power". Especially, in old China, only the king uses the color, and the common people do not have the right to use it. And it also has the other meaning, such as "little" or "young". For examples:

- be draped with the imperial yellow robe by one's supporters 黄袍加身
- a silly little girl 黄毛丫头

But in English, yellow is usually associated with "mean and shameless", "timid and over cautious". For examples:

- yellow dog 忘恩负义之徒
- yellow journalism 耸人听闻的报道
- yellow-bellied 胆小鬼
- My little brother has a yellow streak in him. 我的小兄弟胆怯。

- yellow back 法国的一种廉价小说

3. Green

In English, green is connected with "lacking experiences", "envy" and "being young and vigorous", but in Chinese, the color means "fresh" and "health". For examples：
- a green hand 生手，易上当受骗的人
- green goods 新鲜货
- a green man 新来水手
- a green old age 老当益壮
- We, Chinese youth, should remain forever green like the pine trees. 我们中国青年要始终像松树一样，四季常青，朝气蓬勃。
- She was scared green. 她吓得脸色苍白。
- She is green with envy because my sister has won the prize. 我姐姐得了奖，她非常嫉妒。

4. Blue and Brown

Blue and brown are not used to express feelings of human being in Chinese. But in English, they are connected with "in low spirits". For examples：
- He was in a brown study and took no notice of others' comments. 他陷入深深的思索而丝毫没注意其他人的谈论。
- I felt blue when I failed in the examination. 我考试失败后觉得很沮丧。
- She has left her parents only a week, but she feels homesick and blue. 虽然离开父母仅一周，但她感到思乡且忧郁。

Blue is also used as a commendatory term, which means "well-educated". For examples：
- These ladies are very blue and well-informed. 这些女士都很有知识，很有教养。

5. Black

Both in English and Chinese, black is usually connected with "bad luck" "critical state". For examples：
- She gave me a black look as I passed her. 我经过她身边时她狠狠地瞪了我一眼。
- Every body knows the man is a black villain. 每个人都认为那个人是恶棍。
- Nobody knows why he is always in a black mood. 没人知道他为什么总是那样忧郁。
- He was given a black mark for tardiness. 他因为拖拖拉拉而给人一种不好的印象。

Summary：The different types of color have their different connotative meanings. They cannot be translated according to their conceptual meanings. So we must pay attention to the translation.
- black tea 红茶
- brown sugar 红糖
- brown bread 黑面包

Cultural-loaded Words in Communication   Chapter Seven

- purple wine 红酒
- blue film 色情电影
- green-eyed 眼红
- with red eyes 眼睛哭得发红

7.1.3 Color Words in Economy

In economy life, the color words are also vastly used. There are a great number of phrases and fixed usages which are related to color in economy glossary. The followings are some combined meanings of the color words and some economy words which formed by the color words.

(1) In economy, the word "red" is always related to debt or bankrupt. When the debt income on reckoning is negative, people use red pen to register. Therefore there are phrases like "red figure, red ink, in the red, red-ink entry, and red balance". In addition, usages like red cent, red gold, red tip on stock market are also used frequently.

(2) In English-speaking country, when people talk about "black", it is always related with "bad, evil, and wicked". For example, "black money" means the money with wrong source; "black market" means exchanging things which the government forbids or doing illegal speculated marketing. Except this, "black" can also means payoff. Like red, black is also a kind of color when people keep accounts, such as, "black figure, in the black, black figure nation, interest in the black".

(3) "Blue" in English means unhappy and gloomy. It can also be used to describe the nobles on the upper class; for example, "He is a real blue blood". Another phrase "blue-eyed boys" means the employees on which the management dotes. In economy glossary, blue has many meanings, such as "blue book, blue-sky market, blue-collar workers, and blue chip". "Blue button" means the broker who has the right to enter the stock exchanging. "Blue return" is a kind of table that can only be used by honest taxpayer. "Blue-chip rate" is British favorable credit interest rate. "Blue law" is kind of laws in America which forbid people from doing commercial exchange on Sunday. "Blue-sky law" refers to the law which used to manage the stocks. "Blue sky bargaining" means that the agreement cannot be made because of unpractical request during the negotiation.

(4) In common English "green" always means fresh or envy, but in economy English "green back" is equal to American dollars for the other side of the dollar is green. "Green power" means consortium. "Green meat" means fresh meat. "Green stamp" means the ticket for helping poor people. "Green sheet" is the comparative table of government budget.

(5) White makes one think of immaculacy in English, such as "white war", which means the war without smoke, which always refers to the economy competition. "White goods" refer to the family electric equipments which are big and expensive. Others like

"white money, white coal, white elephant, white sale, the white way" are all useful phrases.

(6) There are still other color words in economy life. "Grey market" means half-black market. "Grey area" means the area where many people lose job. "Pink slip" is the requisition that sends away workers. "Yellow pages" means the classified telephone book.

Questions

1. How does red relate to debt or bankrupt?
2. According to the passage, which color has a negative connotation?
3. What does "blue sky bargaining" mean?
4. Which color indicates the color of U.S. Dollars?
5. Find out the meanings of "white money, white coal, white elephant, white sale, and the white way".

7.2 Proverbs and Idioms

7.2.1 About Proverbs

Proverb is a popular, short sentence stating something commonly experienced or giving advice or warning. It has a memorable form with traditional wisdom, handed down from previous generations. It is short, brief, direct, vivid and taken from daily life. There are three common devices in structuring a proverb.

Alliteration: Practice makes perfect.

Rhyme: Health is better than wealth.

A simple balanced structure: Two is company, three is none; More haste, less speed.

7.2.2 The Proverbs with Similarities of Both English and Chinese Cultures

- A new broom sweeps clean.
- Many hands make light work.
- Don't put off until tomorrow what you can do today.
- Kill two birds with one stone.
- Haste makes waste.
- Where there's smoke, there's fire.
- The grass is always greener on the other side of the fence.
- Beauty is only skin deep.
- Spare the rod and spoil the child.
- Give a person a dose of his own medicine.

7.2.3 Chinese Proverbs without Commonly Known English Equivalents

• 良药苦口利于病,忠言逆耳利于行。

Frank's advice is like good herbal medicine: hard to take, but ultimately beneficial. (Here the bitterness of herbal medicine could only be imagined for some Westerners who have never taken herbal medicine.)

• 瓜田不纳履,李下不正冠。

Neither adjusts your shoes in a melon patch; nor your hat under a plum tree. (If we translate the latter half literally into: "nor straighten your hat beneath an apple tree", it is sure to cause English-speaking people to chuckle, although they might catch the implication immediately.)

7.2.4 English Proverbs without Commonly Known Chinese Equivalents

- Absence makes the heart grow fonder. 越是不见越想念。
- An apple a day keeps the doctor away. 一天一苹果,医生远离我。
- Let sleeping dogs lie. 没惹是非。
- You can't teach an old dog new tricks. 年逾花甲不堪教。
- You can't have your cake and eat it too. 鱼与熊掌不可兼得。

7.2.5 Similarities on the Surface but Differences in the Connotation

• It takes two to make a quarrel——一个巴掌拍不响?

Thinking: The Chinese saying has roughly the same connotation as the English—meaning both people may be at fault. However, the Chinese saying also has another meaning that it often takes more than one person to achieve anything significant.

• A miss is as good as a mile——差之毫厘,谬以千里?

Thinking: The moral often associated with this Chinese expression is a small fault or deviation, if not corrected, will end up in a major error or catastrophe. The Chinese saying is a warning, whereas the English one merely states a fact, or a philosophic attitude that to miss one's mark even very slightly is as bad as missing it by a mile.

• Gilding the lily——锦上添花?

Thinking: English saying implies spoiling something already fine, good or beautiful by attempting to make it better. It expresses an attitude of disapproval, whereas the Chinese one means adding lowers to the brocade, i.e. adding something to make a good thing even better or turning excellence into perfection.

7.2.6 Additional Proverbs

- Soonest done, soonest mended. 捷足者先登。
- Speech is the picture of the mind. 言为心声。
- Go in one ear and out the other. 当作耳旁风；左耳进右耳出。
- Walls have ears. 隔墙有耳。
- To kill the goose that lay the eggs. 杀鸡取卵；竭泽而渔。
- A good dog deserves a good bone. 好狗应该啃好骨头/有功者受赏。
- Barking dogs seldom bite. 爱叫的狗不咬人/咬人的狗不露齿。
- Every dog has his day. 凡人皆有得意日。
- Love me, love my dog. 你若把我当朋友，也要把我的朋友当朋友/爱屋及乌。
- Teach the dog to bark. 教狗怎么叫（意指多此一举）。
- A cat has nine lives. 猫有九条命（英国迷信，指猫的生命力强）。
- A cat in gloves catches no mice. 怕沾污手指的人做不出什么事。
- It's no use crying over spilt milk. 作无意的后悔没有任何作用。
- Where there is smoke there is fire. 无风不起浪。
- Idleness is the root of all evil. 懒散是罪恶的根源。
- As you sow, so you reap. 有耕耘就有收获。
- Live and let live. 待人宽，人亦待己宽。
- A stitch in time saves nine. 小洞不补大洞吃苦。
- 天下没有不散的宴席。All good things must come to an end.
- 众人拾柴火焰高。Many hands make light work.
- 十里不同俗。Other countries, other manners.
- 亲身下河知深浅，亲口尝梨知酸甜。The proof of the pudding is in the eating.
- 甘瓜苦蒂，物无全美。There is no rose without a thorn.

7.3 Culture-loaded Idioms

7.3.1 What's an idiom?

An idiom is a group of words in a fixed order having a particular meaning, different from the meanings of each word understood on its own. It may have the same structure as an ordinary phrase, but it has become frozen in form.

7.3.2 Idioms on Animals

Fill in the blanks with suitable words:

as ____ as a bee   as ____ as a horse
as ____ as an eel   as ____ as a lamb

as _____ as a lark   as _____ as a mule
as _____ as a fox   as _____ as a bat
as _____ as an owl   as _____ as a lion
as _____ as a goose   as _____ as a donkey
as _____ as a cricket   as _____ as a dove

7.4 Numbers

Numbers constitute a special aspect in human language and culture. Numbers are originally the signs for calculating, but they have different connotations under different cultures. The symbolic meanings make the numbers not only mysterious but culturally unique. The comparison between the Chinese and English reflections of the numbers can help us to know the differences in such respects as the psychology, religion and philosophy. Therefore, we can communicate with the English-speakers well.

The differences of colors between China and the western countries mostly come from historical reasons. Chinese worship even numbers but westerners like odd numbers. Historical reasons could date back to the books written in ancient times like *The Bible* in western countries and *The Book of Changes*(易经) in China, which play an important role in the formation of different concept of colors.

7.4.1 Different Cultures in Numbers

1. Seven

Seven is considered as a nice number in English. But in Chinese it has both sides. Seven has a great relation with the religion. The Bible records that the God used seven days to create human beings, and in Christianity there are seven virtues.

- be in seventh heaven 非常幸福,非常快乐
- the Boeing Company: 737, 747, 757, 767, 777
- Seven Up 七喜
- Mild Seven(香烟)柔和七星,万事发

In Buddhism, there are also the sayings like the story that Sakyamuni sitting forty nine days meaning seven multiply seven, and then becoming a Buddha. The worship of seven is derived from astronomy; it has close relation with the Big Dipper, which consists of seven stars. Seven is defined as the sum of Yin and Yang and Wu Xing in Chinese, so it means harmony in Confucianism. However, the pronunciation of it in Chinese is not good, so seven is related to death often. And nowadays, the bad side is mentioned more than the good side.

2. Four vs. Thirteen

The Chinese like the even numbers, except 4, due to the same pronunciation with death in Chinese. Sometimes there is no 4th room in the hotel. Many Chinese people do not want

their telephone number to have 4. Four also has some good meanings, for examples:
- one who is forty without doubt 四十而不惑
- be dependable 四平八稳
- extend in all directions 四通八达

"13" comes across the same condition in western countries as "4" in China. There is no 13th floor in their buildings. Because of the story in Bible, which says that the day when Eve and Adam eat the drug apple is 13, then the number becomes the worst number in the Western people's hearts. As we all know, Friday is a bad day, and if people meet "13" and Friday in the same day, they will think it the worst day.

7.5 Taboos

7.5.1 Naming Taboo

In China naming taboo is a cultural taboo against speaking or writing the given names of noble persons.

1. The Naming Taboo of the "State"（国讳）

It discouraged the use of the emperor's given name and those of his ancestors. During the Qin Dynasty, Qin Shi Huang's given name Zheng（政）was avoided, and the first month of the year Zheng Yue（政月：the administrative month）was rewritten into Zheng Yue（正月：the upright month）and furthermore renamed as Duan Yue（端月：the proper/upright month）. The character 正 was also pronounced Zeng instead of Zheng to avoid any similarity.

Generally, ancestor names going back to seven generations were avoided. The strength of this taboo was reinforced by law. The violation of the law would result in the violator and his family's executions and confiscation of their property.

2. The Naming Taboo of the "Clan"（家讳）

It discouraged the use of the names of one's own ancestors. In diplomatic documents and letters between clans, each clan's naming taboos were observed. The naming taboo of the "holiness"（圣人讳）discouraged the use of the names of respected people. For example, writing Confucius' name was a taboo during the Jin Dynasty.

In western countries, there is no such a thing as naming taboo of the state or the clan. People could call each other's given names directly to show equality, intimacy and friendliness.

In English, taboos on the names of gods include taboos on the name of God, of Jesus Christ, of Saint Mary, of Satan, etc. For the people who believe in Christianity, God exists everywhere, and the name of God and other words connected with religion can only be used in the religious situations. In other situations, those words are taboos. So people usually use "gosh" "golly" to refer to God.

The English also has taboos on the name of Satan who is an evil and the opponent of God. They do not refer to the name of Satan directly, because they think "Speaking of the devil, it is sure to appear." People usually call Satan "the Evil One" "the Common Enemy" and so on.

7.5.2 Taboos on Death

1. Chinese Taboos on Death

For death is all man's destiny, Chinese people hope for longevity, and death that follows longevity is considered as a blessing. For example, people use"驾鹤,仙逝,圆寂" (for the Buddhist monks) to indicate the death of those people with longevity.

2. English Taboos on Death

Similarly, western people rarely talk openly about death. When people have to talk about it, they usually use euphemisms, such as "pass away; pass out; close one's days; fall asleep forever; join great majority; pay the debt of nature; depart to God; be in heaven."

7.5.3 How to Avoid Taboo—Using Euphemisms

In Western culture:
- street cleaner（清洁工）—environmental beautician（环境美容师）
- hospital nurse（护士）—angle in white（白衣天使）
- postman（邮递员）—messenger in green（绿衣使者）
- Jesus/Jesus Christ—Jeeze/Gee
- My God — My goodness
- be sent to prison —be sent to the big houses
- wash one's hands / powder one's nose / spend a penny —go to the WC

In Chinese culture:
- 更衣、办公—上厕所
- 吃双份饭—怀孕
- 孩子他爹—丈夫
- 发福、富态—胖

7.6 Review Tasks

Ⅰ. Decide whether the following statements are true (T) or false (F).

1. "Dragon" means the same to the westerner as "龙" to the Chinese. (　)
2. The Chinese phrase "知识分子" has the same meaning as "intellectual". (　)
3. A term in one language may not have a counterpart in another language. (　)
4. There are as many similarities as dissimilarities between English proverbs and

Chinese proverbs. ( )

5. Using euphemism is a very good way to avoid taboos in both Chinese and English cultures. ( )

6. In western countries, there is no such a thing as naming taboo of the state or the clan. ( )

7. If Chinese people meet "13" and Friday in the same day, they will think it the worst day. ( )

8. Chinese people do not want their telephone number to have 4 due to religious reason. ( )

9. The number "7" is preferred by Chinese because many Chinese people prefer odd number. ( )

10. The differences of colors between China and the Western countries mostly come from historical reasons. ( )

11. An idiom is a group of words in a fixed order having a particular meaning. It never has the same structure as an ordinary phrase. ( )

12. Red in Western culture symbolizes good luck, happiness and progress. ( )

13. In English, yellow is usually associated with "mean and shameless" "timid and over cautious". ( )

14. In English, "a white man" means a dishonest and cunning man. ( )

15. In Chinese, green is connected with "lacking experiences" "envy" and "being young and vigorous". ( )

16. Blue and brown are not used to express feelings of human being in English. But in Chinese, they are connected with "in low spirits". ( )

17. In Chinese and English culture, "Black market" means exchanging things which the government forbids or doing illegal speculated marketing. ( )

18. In common English "green" always means fresh or envy, but in economy English "green back" is equal to American dollars. ( )

19. Culture-loaded words are the vocabulary which can best embody the cultural information that a language carries. ( )

20. In ancient China, naming taboo is a cultural taboo against speaking or writing the family names of noble persons. ( )

Ⅱ. **Give the Chinese equivalents of the following proverbs and idioms.**

1. Justice has long arms.
2. Diamond cut diamond.
3. Golden saying
4. Fat office
5. You will cross the bridge when you get to it.
6. Better be the head of a dog than the tail of a lion.
7. Drink like a fish.

Cultural-loaded Words in Communication

8. Tread upon eggs.

III. Translate the following statements and pay attention to the numbers.

1. At sixes and sevens
2. On second thoughts
3. By ones and twos
4. Two heads are better than one.
5. —Can you come down a little?
   —Sorry, it's one price for all.
6. —Are you taking Pam out tonight?
   —Ah, that's the sixty-four-thousand dollar question!
7. He had one over the eight after he drank only half bottle of the wine.
8. Ten to one he has forgotten it.

IV. Analyze the following cases and answer the questions.

Case one

Ted, an American student met his Chinese classmate Liu Dan.

Ted: Hi Dan, I have a question. The other day I was trying to buy a hat at this mall, the shop assistant giggled when I was trying on the green one. She doesn't speak much English, so I thought about asking you.

Dan: Well, here's a little tip for men in China hoping to avoid public castigation: don't wear a green hat. Because...

Ted: This advice came a little late for me. But roger that.

Dan: I noticed that colors do have different connotations in English. Can you think of any examples since you've been here for almost one semester?

Ted: Yeah, I do have one in mind. The other day I saw a battery brand called "White Elephant". I was thinking "this won't sell in the U.S."...

Questions

1. Can you help Liu Dan finish his explanation on "green hat" to his friend Ted?
2. Please find out the connotation of "white elephant" and share with your class.

Case two

Here are two cases about numbers in different cultural backgrounds:

(1) It is said that American President Franklin Roosevelt always avoided leaving on trips on the thirteen of the month. He would hastily invite his private secretary to attend a meal or a meeting just to avoid thirteen at the table.

(2) The opening ceremony of Beijing 2008 Olympic Games started at 20:00 China Standard Time on Friday, 8 August 2008.

Questions

1. What is the connotation of number 13 in Western culture?

2. How are you going to explain to your international friends about the connotation of number 8 in Chinese culture?

V. Extended Reading.

Passage one

Color Psychology

Color psychology is the study of hues as a determinant of human behavior. Color influences perceptions that are not obvious, such as the taste of food. Colors can also work as placebos by having the color of pills with certain colors to influence how a person feels after taking them. For example, red or orange pills are generally used as stimulants. Another way in which colors have been used to influence behavior was, in 2000, when the company Glasgow installed blue street lights in certain neighborhoods which resulted in a reduced crime rate. Color can indeed influence a person; however, it is important to remember that these effects differ between people. Factors such as gender, age, and culture can influence how an individual perceives color. For example, males reported that red colored outfits made women seem more attractive, while women answered that the color of a male's outfit did not affect his attractiveness.

Color psychology is also widely used in marketing and branding. Many marketers see color as an important part of marketing because color can be used to influence consumers' emotions and perceptions of goods and services. Companies also use color when deciding on brand logos. These logos seem to attract more customers when the color of the brand logo matches the personality of the goods or services, such as the color pink being heavily used on Victoria's Secret branding. However, colors are not only important for logos and products, but also for window displays in stores. Research shows that warm colors tended to attract spontaneous purchasers, despite cooler colors being more favorable.

(https://en.wikipedia.org/wiki/Color_psychology)

Questions

1. Can you sum up the examples that the passage touches upon on color psychology?

2. "Factors such as gender, age, and culture can influence how an individual perceives color." Please brainstorm some other examples to support this statement in the passage.

Passage two

Color Preference and Associations between Color and Mood

Color has long been used to create feelings of coziness or spaciousness. However, how people are affected by different color stimuli varies from person to person.

Cultural-loaded Words in Communication

Blue is the top choice for 35% of Americans, followed by green (16%), purple (10%) and red (9%). A preference for blue and green may be due to a preference for certain habitats that were beneficial in the ancestral environment as explained in the evolutionary aesthetics article.

There is evidence that color preference may depend on ambient temperature. People who are cold prefer warm colors like red and yellow while people who are hot prefer cool colors like blue and green. Some research has concluded that women and men respectively prefer "warm" and "cool" colors. A few studies have shown that cultural background has a strong influence on color preference. These studies have shown that people from the same region regardless of race will have the same color preferences. Also, one region may have different preferences than another region (i.e., a different country or a different area of the same country), regardless of race.

Children's preferences for colors they find to be pleasant and comforting can be changed and can vary, while adult color preference is usually non-malleable. Some studies find that color can affect mood. However, these studies do not agree on precisely which moods are brought out by which colors.

A study by psychologist Andrew J. Elliot tested to see if the color of a person's clothing could make them appear more sexually appealing. He found that to men, women dressed in the color red were significantly more likely to attract romantic attention than women in any other color. However, for women, the color of one's shirt made no difference in their level of attractiveness.

Despite cross-cultural differences regarding what different colors meant there were cross-cultural similarities regarding what emotional states people associated with different colors in one study. For example, the color red was perceived as strong and active.

(Adapted from https://en.wikipedia.org)

Questions

1. Do you agree that color can affect mood?
2. After reading this passage, do you think people's perception on colors is more associated with cultural differences or individual differences?

Chapter Eight
Intercultural Communication Competence

> *Tolerance for each other's difference is the only way we can survive.*
> —Whoopi Goldberg
>
> *As the traveler who has once been away from home is wiser than one who has never left his own doorstep, a knowledge of one other culture should sharpen our ability to scrutinize more steadily, to appreciate more lovingly, our own.*
> —Margaret Mead

When we study something, we want to know not only what it is, but also why and how it is so. This is very true of culture. In this chapter, we will identify some whys and hows in the study of intercultural communication.

8.1 Aware of Cultural Value Differences

We all know that there are many differences between distinct cultures, but why is this so since we are basically the same human beings with basically the same needs for food, dressing, shelter, security, love, esteem, etc.? Why do some cultures frantically cling to youth, whereas others welcome old age? Why do some cultures worship the Earth, whereas others molest it? Why is it that in some cultures independence is emphasized while in others interdependence is preferred? There is no end to such questions. In seeking the answers, we should understand and be well aware of the cultural value differences in order to better adapt to another new culture and conduct successful intercultural communication.

8.1.1 Instruments of Comparing Cultural Values

Cultural differences are usually where misunderstandings and even conflicts may arise when peoples of different cultural backgrounds meet, so it is essential to compare the similarities and differences, which is a very effective way to increase and deepen the

Intercultural Communication Competence

understanding of our life and the world. To compare, we need some instruments. Scholars have proposed different frames of cultural comparison. In this part we will present two classifications developed by Kluchhohn and Hofstede respectively. Hopefully the classifications will help us have a deeper understanding of different cultures and become better intercultural communicators.

Kluchhohn's value orientations

Value orientations are complex but definitely patterned principles which give order and direction to human acts and thoughts as these relate to the solution of "common human problems". The American anthropologist Clyde Kluchhohn and social psychologist Fred Strodtbeck list five problems for which all cultures must find solutions. Posed as questions, these problems are as follows:

(1) What is the inborn character of human nature?
(2) What is the relationship between people and nature?
(3) What is the focus of human life with respect to time?
(4) What is the focus of human activity?
(5) What is the relationship of one person to another?

1. Human-Nature Orientation

The traditional Western belief about human nature is that humans are basically evil. We may see this in *The Bible* about the story of Adam and Eve. God threw them out of the Garden of Eden because they ate the fruit from the Tree of Knowledge. Since then, according to Christian teaching, all human beings have been born with original sin. People have to try to perfect their nature by keeping doing good things. The distrust of human nature can be seen in American political institutions with their checks and balances.

In contrast, the Asian people who have accepted Confucianism believe that human beings are basically good. The very typical embodiment of this idea is the Three Character Classic that begins with "Man, by nature, is good; people's inborn characters are similar, but learning makes them different"(人之初,性本善。性相近,习相远). There are many stories and teachings on this point, such as the story of Mencius's mother moving three times in order that her son could be in a good neighborhood, and the saying that "Your character will be tinted 'red' if you are in the company of 'redness', but 'black' if you are in close contact with ink"(近朱者赤,近墨者黑).

2. Man-Nature Orientation

Chinese believe that man should live in harmony with nature. The philosophy holds that a "power" links all things and creatures together. This cooperation view is found in Chinese medicine, architecture, proverbs, etc. Typical Chinese gardens and houses reveal their social attitudes towards the relationship between humans and nature. Pavilions, paved pathways, and other structures are integrated with natural features of water, trees and rock. There is no sharp distinction between being inside a building and being outside in nature.

The Western experience of human life being separate from nature can be found in the Biblical story of creation. When God created Adam, he was given dominance over all of God's creation. As masters of nature, humans are encouraged to control and exploit it in any way they choose. This view (man being separated from nature) has contributed to the development of Western science and technology. But today more and more Westerners have come to realize that mastery-over-nature philosophy causes problems and humans should protect the environment.

3. Time Orientation

Cultures vary widely in their conceptions of time. Where they differ is in the value placed on the past, the present, and the future and how each influences interaction. Past-oriented people tend to believe tradition is important. To them, the cultural memory is rich and deep. They like to look back to a period when their culture was at the height of its power and glory and may quote respected philosophers and leaders from the past as a guide for action in the present. They may feel more secure when something new is defined as similar to something that occurred in the past. Asian cultures including the Chinese are believed to hold this orientation.

Present-oriented cultures maintain that the moment is of the most significance. For them, the future is vague, ambiguous and unknown, and what is real exists in the here and now. Samovar et al state that people of the Philippines, Mexico and Latin America usually have this belief.

If you tend to look to the future and make plans for the future, you are future-oriented. Cultures with this orientation tend to emphasize the future and expect it to be grander and nicer than the present. Whether the future is seen as probably good or not, future-oriented people tend to see time as a straight line that leads from the past and that is swiftly moving into the future. In other words, time is a linear concept.

4. Activity Orientation

This orientation is the way a culture views activity. Three common modes of activity expression are being, being-in-coming, and doing.

In being-oriented cultures, people are satisfied with what they are, and family background is more important than what they accomplish. Their actions express who they are. For that reason people behave in ways appropriate to their positions (status, social roles, and character) in life.

Being-in-becoming orientations often correlate with cultures that value a spiritual life more than a material life. For instance, in both Hinduism and Buddhism, people spend a great portion of their lives in meditation and contemplation in an attempt to purify and more fully advance themselves. For them, this inner or spiritual development represents one of the main purposes of life.

Doing orientation leads to external accomplishments. The goal is to achieve as much as possible. You want to do things and to achieve success, so you tend to be more active. Because the emphasis is on action in doing culture, the goals towards which action is directed are also emphasized. There is often a sense of urgency about getting things done. Deadlines are important, as is the schedule. To have a full schedule indicates that you are accomplishing things.

5. Relational Orientation

This value orientation is concerned with the ways in which people perceive their relationships with others. There are three types concerning this orientation: hierarchy, group, and individual. In fact, any society consists of hierarchies. The difference is whether and how much hierarchy is emphasized or deemphasized. In a hierarchy people have clearly defined privileges and obligations according to their positions, but hierarchical societies differ from one another depending on the criteria used to assign a person a place in the hierarchy. If the criteria are related to race, ethnic group, or inheritance from one's parents, then the hierarchy may be rigid and unchanging with certain groups permanently on the top and others permanently at the bottom.

In societies where relationships are based on groups, each person's social identity comes from their group memberships. People feel dependent on the group, safe within it, proud and competitive with other groups. Loyalty is important in group-oriented cultures. In this pattern the group act out of concern for all its members and make decisions by consensus, and members are loyal to the group.

In individualistic societies, social relations are based on the autonomy of each person. There are some hierarchies in individualistic cultures, but people are uncomfortable with them and try to communicate with one another in a way that denies their existence or reduces their impact. For example, people prefer to use first names; high-ranking people send messages that they are just like everyone else. People tend to be less aware of others' feelings and may talk more than people from group-oriented cultures. Self-reliance and independence are important and it is considered weak to be dependent on others.

Hofstede's value orientations

The influential Dutch expert on intercultural communication Geert Hofstede has identified four value dimensions that have a significant impact on behavior in all cultures. These dimensions are individualism and collectivism, uncertainty avoidance, power distance, and masculinity and femininity.

1. Individualism and Collectivism

The individual is the single most important unit in any social setting, regardless of the size of that unit, and the uniqueness of each individual is of great value. Individualistic cultures give more importance to individual's needs when they do things such as setting goals. According to Hofstede's findings, the United States, Australia, Great Britain, Canada and New Zealand tend towards individualism.

Collectivism is characterized by a rigid social framework that distinguishes between in-groups and out-groups. People count on their in-group (relatives, clans, organizations) to look after them, and in exchange for that they believe they owe absolute loyalty to the group.

2. Uncertainty Avoidance

Uncertainty avoidance deals with the degree to which members of a culture try to avoid uncertainty. In comparison to members of cultures low in uncertainty avoidance, members of cultures high in uncertainty avoidance have a lower tolerance for uncertainty and ambiguity, which expresses itself in higher levels of anxiety, greater need for formal rules and absolute truth, and less tolerance for people or groups with different ideas or behaviors. Members of high uncertainty avoidance cultures also tend to display emotions more than members of low uncertainty avoidance cultures. Members of low uncertainty avoidance cultures have lower stress levels and accept different ideas and taking risks more than members of high uncertainty avoidance cultures.

Uncertainty avoidance is useful in understanding differences in how strangers are treated. People in high uncertainty avoidance cultures try to avoid ambiguity and, therefore, develop rules and rituals for virtually every possible situation. Interaction with strangers in cultures high in uncertainty avoidance may be highly ritualistic and/or very polite.

3. Power Distance

Power distance is "the extent to which the less powerful members of institutions and organizations accept that power is distributed unequally." Hofstede is not trying to measure how unequally people actually are in a particular culture. He is trying to measure how equal or unequal the people in a particular culture think people should be. Individuals from high power distance cultures accept power as part of society. As a result, superiors consider their subordinates to be different from themselves and vice versa. Members of low power distance cultures believe power should be used only when it is legitimate and prefer expert or legitimate power.

Power distance is useful in understanding strangers' behavior in role relationships, particularly those involving different degrees of power or authority. People from high power distance cultures, for example, do not question their superiors' orders. They expect to be told what to do. People in low power distance cultures, in contrast, do not necessarily accept superiors' orders readily; they want to know why they should follow them. When people from two different systems interact, misunderstanding is likely unless one or both understand the other person's system.

4. Masculinity and Femininity

The major differentiation between masculinity and femininity cultures is how gender roles are distributed in cultures.

Hofstede points out that in masculine cultures, social gender roles are clearly distinct.

Men are supposed to be assertive, tough, and focused on material success whereas women are supposed to be more modest, tender and concerned with quality of life.

In feminine cultures social gender roles overlap. In these cultures, no one should fight and no one should be too ambitious. Everyone should be concerned with maintaining good relationships with others. Both men and women are supposed to be modest, tender and concerned with the quality of life.

Hofstede points out that in masculine cultures, people have stronger motivation for achievement, view work as more central to their lives, accept the company's "interference" in their private lives, have higher job stress, have greater value differences between men and women in the same position, and view recognition, advancement and challenges more important than their satisfaction with their work. In masculine cultures, women are assigned the role of being tender and taking care of relationships. In feminine cultures, in contrast, both men and women engage in these behaviors. Fathers and mothers are expected to deal with children together. Employees in organizations "live in order to work" in masculine cultures and "work in order to live" in feminine cultures. Members of masculine cultures focus on ego enhancement and members of feminine cultures focus on relationship enhancement.

Masculinity-femininity is useful in understanding cultural differences in opposite-sex and same-sex relationships. People from highly masculine cultures, for example, tend to have little contact with members of the opposite-sex when they grow up. They tend to see same-sex relationships as more intimate than opposite-sex relationships. As to people from a feminine culture, they may communicate effectively with strangers from a masculine culture, for they understand each other's orientation towards sex-roles.

8.2 Adapting to a New Culture

8.2.1 Culture Shock

What is culture shock? Culture shock can be described as the feeling of confusion and disorientation that one experiences when facing with a large number of new and unfamiliar people and situations. Many things contribute to it — smell, sounds, flavors, the very feeling of the air one is breathing. Of course, the unfamiliar language and behavior of the native people contribute to it, too. People's responses to culture shock vary greatly, from excitement and energetic action to withdrawal, depression, physical illness, and hostility.

8.2.2 Stages of Culture Shock

Stage 1: Honeymoon Stage

Like any new experience, the newcomer is usually excited to be in the new country.

Everything is exciting, stimulating. People are friendly and the future is full of promise. This is where one will overlook minor problems and look forward to learning new things.

Stage 2: Rejection Stage

In this stage, everything no longer feels new; in fact, it's starting to feel like a thick wall preventing you from experiencing things. Gradually, one starts refusing to accept the differences one encounters, and realizes that familiar support systems are not easily accessible. The negative feelings such as loneliness, depression, sense of loss, or even hostility usually appear during this time.

Stage 3: Adjustment Stage

One is more familiar with the new environment and develops routines through adjusting and establishing an objective. One becomes concerned with basic living again, starts to develop problem-solving skills to deal with the culture differences, and begins to accept the culture ways with a positive attitude. The culture turns to make sense, and negative reactions and responses to the culture are reduced.

Stage 4: Acceptance Stage

One will feel at home and become involved in activities and may enjoy some of that country's customs. One starts to accept the differences and feel like one can begin to live with natives. A feeling of confidence in better coping with any problems may arise. One no longer feels isolated, and instead demonstrates an increased interest and ability to relax and enjoy the host culture.

Stage 5: Reentry Stage

This is experienced upon returning to the home country and the return may follow with initial euphoria, crisis or disenchantment. It may be hard to readjust and may feel one is not accepted. He/she feels different about the same thing from the original country when one returns. For instance, the taste of food seems different from that of used to be; the city where he/she had grown up is more crowded than before, etc.

8.2.3 Strategies for Avoiding Culture Shock

If you are traveling to a new culture for the first time, it is likely that you will experience some kind of culture shock or intercultural adaptation. The level of intensity you experience will vary. In addition, the duration of your culture shock and degree of your intercultural adaptation will depend on your ability to manage it. Successful management of culture shock depends on an awareness of its symptoms and the degree of its severity. Therefore, keep in mind that everyone experiences some degree of culture shock when entering a new culture for some length of time. However, if managed appropriately, most culture shock is significantly reduced after about one year. At the same time and also after that, you can try to engage yourself into the intercultural adaptation.

(1) Study the host culture.

(2) Study the local environment.

(3) Learn basic verbal and nonverbal language skills.
(4) Develop intercultural relationships.
(5) Maintain an intimate social network.
(6) Assume the principle of difference.
(7) Anticipate future events.

8.3 Improving Intercultural Communication Competence

8.3.1 Definition of Intercultural Communication Competence (ICC)

In contemporary world of global village, intercultural communication has become increasingly important. As we know, communication, language and culture cannot be separated. Successful intercultural communication demands linguistic fluency, cultural fluency as well as communication competence.

Besides the fundamental learning of language itself, we should also be aware of and sensitive to the culturally determined patterns of verbal and nonverbal communication which speakers of the target culture follow. Communication competence is a social judgment that people make about others. The judgment depends on the context, the relationship between the communicators; the goals or objectives that the communicators want to achieve, and the specific verbal and nonverbal messages that are used to accomplish these goals.

Intercultural communication competence is a part of communication competence. Myron W. Lustig and Jolene Koester, American famous experts on communication, defined "intercultural competence" as "the ability to become effective and appropriate in interacting across cultures". It is the ability to understand and adapt to the target culture without ignoring the native culture. It also refers to the sensitivity to cultural diversity.

Therefore, intercultural communication competence refers to the ability to accomplish effective and appropriate intercultural communication between communicators of different cultures. In short, it is often written as "ICC".

8.3.2 Strategies for Improving Intercultural Communication Competence

There are a large body of research regarding strategies for improving intercultural competence, among which one classification is introduced in this book, in terms of intercultural competency factors, which are associated with intercultural effectiveness, such as ethnocentrism, cognitive complexity, self-esteem and confidence, innovativeness, trust in people, and acculturation motivation.

1. Ethnocentrism

In a series of investigations it has been proved that highly ethnocentric individuals are less likely to adjust well during a transitional experience. In fact, prejudice and ethnocentrism are difficult barriers and often block adequate cultural adjustment and relationship formation in cultures; therefore, it is important to control the effects of criticism of the new culture as well as negative attitudes towards the new culture because this will hinder intercultural effectiveness.

2. Cognitive Complexity

Cognitive complexity refers to the ability of a person to perceive a wide variety of things about another person and to make finer interpersonal discrimination than cognitively simple individuals. People who can see a variety of things about another person in contrast to seeing only limited details usually experience greater intercultural effectiveness. In general, cognitively complex individuals make better and more accurate judgments in developing impressions about others. They see more possibilities about people and situations.

3. Self-esteem and Confidence

Both self-esteem and confidence foster intercultural effectiveness. Indeed, self-confidence and initiative directly correlate with personal adjustment and performance. Everyone has self doubts once in a while, and fear can freeze our emotions and spirits. At the root of some fear is low self-esteem. Beyond those momentary losses of confidence, however, most of us can really perform beyond our expectations.

4. Innovativeness

Innovativeness is also a factor that contributes to intercultural effectiveness. Innovativeness means the ability to make significant strides in developing and accepting new ideas; a willingness to experiment with new approaches and especially a willingness to learn.

5. Trust in people

Trust in people also helps to build strong and healthy interpersonal relationships, enabling one to develop intercultural competence. Researchers have correlated trust in people with intercultural effectiveness and found this variable to be an important predictor.

6. Acculturation Motivation

The desire to learn the language, become knowledgeable about the culture, and adapt within a new culture is correlated with successful acculturation. It is the first factor influencing our intercultural effectiveness.

8.4 An Integration of Eastern and Western Culture

1. Synthesis

To summarize, many differences between the two cultures stem fundamentally from their respective thoughts on the reality of the universe, nature, knowledge, time, and communication. Based on an organic, holistic, and cyclic view, the East has developed an epistemology that emphasizes direct immediate and aesthetic components in human nature's experience of the world. The ultimate aim of human learning is to be spiritually united with the universe and to find eternity within the recent moment. The Western culture, based on dualism, determinism, and materialism, encourages an outlook that is rational, analytic and direct. History is viewed as a linear progression from the past to the future.

These different world views, in turn, have been reflected in the individual conception of self, others, and the group. While the East has stressed the primacy of the group over the individual, the West has stressed the primacy of the individual over the group.

Of course, the differences are not in diametric opposition; rather, they are differences in emphasis. The contributions the west has made to the material development far exceeds the historical learning of the East. However, the aesthetic and holistic view of the East offers a deeper understanding of human experience, the natural world, and the universe compared to the Western view.

Thus, the Eastern and Western cultures are not contradictory in essence, but are, instead, intensely complementary. The values, behaviors, and institutions of the West should not be substituted for their Eastern counterparts, and vice versa. Our task is not to trade one view for another but to integrate them. The purpose of evolution is not to create a homogeneous mass, but to gradually unfold a diverse yet organic whole.

2. Complementarity

The wide spectrum of our everyday life activities demands both scientific and aesthetic modes of apprehension: from critical analysis to perception of wholes; from doubt and skepticism to unconditional appreciation; from abstraction to correctness; and from the general and regular to the individual and unique. If we limit ourselves to the traditional Western scientific mode of apprehension or if we do not value and practice the Eastern aesthetic mode, we are limiting the essential human to only a part of the full span of life activities.

One potential benefit of incorporating the Eastern aesthetic orientation into Western life is a heightened sense of freedom. The Eastern view would also bring the Westerners a heightened awareness that the universe is alive. Moreover, the holistic, aesthetic component in human nature and in the nature of all things pacifies us, so another potential benefit of incorporating the Western functional, pragmatic interpersonal orientation into Eastern life is the drive for growth in material progress and social change.

8.5 Review Tasks

Ⅰ. **Decide whether the following statements are true (T) or false (F).**

1. The reason why we should be aware of cultural value differences is that we need to

find better substitute to the present cultural patterns. ( )

2. In order to compare the similarities and differences of cultural values, we should find some instruments of comparison to have a deeper understanding. ( )

3. According to Kluchhohn, there are five orientations in which Eastern and Western cultural patterns are sharply different. ( )

4. The traditional Eastern belief about human nature is that humans are basically evil. ( )

5. Past-oriented people may feel more secure when something new is defined as similar to something that occurred in the past. ( )

6. Cultures with present orientation tend to emphasize the future and expect it to be grander and nicer than the present. ( )

7. Doing orientations often correlate with cultures that value a spiritual life more than a material life. ( )

8. According to Kluchhohn, there are three types concerning relational orientation: hierarchy, group, and family. ( )

9. According to Hofstede, members of high uncertainty avoidance cultures have lower stress levels and accept different ideas and taking risks less than members of low uncertainty avoidance cultures. ( )

10. In feminine cultures, according to Hofstede, women are usually assigned the role of being tender and taking care of relationships. ( )

11. Successful management of culture shock depends on an awareness of its symptoms and the degree of its severity. ( )

12. Insomnia can be one example of the symptoms of culture shock. ( )

13. The duration of your culture shock and degree of your intercultural adaptation will largely depend on your own personality. ( )

14. Only people of very poor intercultural competence experience some degree of culture shock when entering a new culture for some length of time. ( )

15. Successful intercultural communication demands linguistic fluency, cultural fluency as well as communication competence. ( )

16. The differences between the East and the West are not in diametric opposition; rather, they are differences in emphasis. ( )

17. One of the strategies for improving intercultural communication competence is to develop ethnocentrism. ( )

18. Both self-esteem and confidence foster intercultural effectiveness. ( )

19. The Eastern and Western cultures are contradictory in essence, so it is impossible to integrate both. ( )

20. One potential benefit of incorporating Eastern and Western orientation is the drive for growth in material progress and social change. ( )

Intercultural Communication Competence — Chapter Eight

II. Discuss the following questions.

1. What are the instruments to compare cultural values?
2. What is "culture shock"? And how to avoid or overcome culture shock?
3. What is "intercultural communication competence" and how to improve our ICC?

III. Analyze the following cases and answer the questions.

Case one

When an American student enters China, he feels that all or most of his familiar cues in his culture are removed. And he feels that he is like a fish out of water. No matter how broad-minded or full of good will he may be, he feels out of place in his new environment. This is followed by a feeling of frustration and anxiety. He reacts to the frustration by rejecting the environment which causes the discomfort. "I'm not able to adapt to the Chinese ways, because they make me feel discomfortable."

Questions

1. Why does the student feel that he is like a fish out of water?
2. Do you think his feeling of frustration and anxiety is reasonable?
3. So do you think his reaction to the problem is suitable? If you experience such situations, what will your responses be?

Case two

When traveling San Francisco and then visiting its Chinatown, you can find there are lots of signs in Chinese and people there speaking Chinese. And also many street signs in other US cities such as New York, Miami, or Honolulu, are in another language in addition to English.

Questions

1. What kind of cultural phenomenon can be reflected in this case?

147

2. Could you give some examples of phenomena similar to this one in American society?

Case three

Swedes tend to think that Americans are superficial and openly proud of themselves because they talk a lot. Swedes generally don't mind silence. If you pause for a while before answering a question or saying something about the topic being discussed, to a Swede that means you find the question or topic important and you are thinking before you talk. It also tells a Swede that you're intelligent.

Also, Swedes don't like it when people talk about how good they are at something. You may be good at something, but you're supposed to deny it and say you need to learn more or something like that. And don't interrupt!

If someone offers you a gift, it would be suitable to seem a bit embarrassed or moved, and always offer to pay for your meal if you go out together.

Americans are always surprised when I say I think American women are not very liberated. In Sweden, men on the average do 40% of the house work. Younger men do more, and older men do less. In the U.S. men can't stay home with their babies. In the U.S., you find more women in top executive positions but it seems they had to give up a lot to get there.

Question

Think about what other clues this passage suggests that help us understand intercultural communication.

IV. Extended Reading.

Cross-cultural Competence

Cross-cultural competence (3C) has generated confusing and contradictory definitions because it has been studied by a wide variety of academic approaches and professional fields. One author identified eleven different terms that have some equivalence to 3C: cultural savvy, astuteness, appreciation, literacy or fluency, adaptability, terrain, expertise, competency, awareness, intelligence, and understanding. The United States Army Research Institute, which is currently engaged in a study of 3C, has defined it as "A set of cognitive, behavioral, and affective/motivational components that enable individuals to adapt effectively in intercultural environments."

Organizations in academia, business, health care, government security, and developmental aid agencies have all sought to use 3C in one way or another. Poor results have often been obtained due to a lack of rigorous study of 3C and a reliance on "common sense" approaches.

Cross-cultural competence does not operate in a vacuum, however. One theoretical construct posits that 3C, language proficiency, and regional knowledge are distinct skills that are inextricably linked, but to varying degrees depending on the context in which they

Intercultural Communication Competence   Chapter Eight

are employed. In educational settings, Bloom's affective and cognitive taxonomies serve as an effective framework for describing the overlapping areas among these three disciplines: at the receiving and knowledge levels, 3C can operate with near-independence from language proficiency and regional knowledge. But, as one approaches the internalizing and evaluation levels, the overlapping areas approach totality.

The development of intercultural competence is mostly based on the individual's experiences while he or she is communicating with different cultures. When interacting with people from other cultures, the individual experiences certain obstacles that are caused by differences in cultural understanding between two people from different cultures. Such experiences may motivate the individual to acquire skills that can help him to communicate his point of view to an audience belonging to a different cultural ethnicity and background.

(*Adapted from https://en.wikipedia.org*)

Question

Why is it necessary to develop cross-cultural competence?

149

Keys to Review Tasks

Chapter One　Culture and Communication

I. Decide whether the following statements are true (T) or false (F).

1. F 2. T 3. T 4. T 5. F 6. T 7. T 8. F 9. T 10. T 11. F 12. F 13. T 14. F 15. T 16. F 17. F 18. T 19. F 20. T

II. Discuss the following questions.

(Suggested answers)

1. Communication is a dynamic, systematic process in which meanings are created and reflected in human interaction with symbols. Communication is central to our existence. Our experiences tell us that communication is closely connected with our everyday life; without it we can hardly survive.

2. Culture generally refers to a shared background (e.g. national, ethnic, religious) resulting from a common language and communication style, customs, beliefs, attitudes, and values. It includes the informal and often hidden patterns of human interactions, expressions, and viewpoints that people in one culture share. Miscommunication, misunderstanding and even conflict may occur if we know nothing about culture of others as well as our own. In that case we cannot achieve development and harmony in the world.

3. Communication permeates our life, and our life is guided by our cultures. Communication itself is the basic human need, but the way an individual communicates emanates from his or her culture.

III. Analyze the following cases and answer the questions.

Case one

(Suggested answers)

1. The American regarded that her Japanese friend belittled the husband of herself as a lack of confidence and this would be shrugged off in the Western culture.

2. This is just a formulaic polite expression to show her modesty, which commonly happened in the Eastern culture.

Case two

(Suggested answers)

1. The originality is more important than the repetition of others' opinion.

2. He might tell his lecturer what he had paid for the essay in order to defend himself.

IV. Extended Reading.

Passage one

(Suggested answers)

1. study the history of the other cultures; learn the nonverbal language used by other cultures; understand different attitudes towards "saving face"; recognize different perceptions of time; avoid rushes to judgment; continually practice.

2. A same nonverbal communication form may contain different meanings according to different cultural backgrounds, so its meaning will be possibly developed or even changed by cultures.

Passage two

(Suggested answers)

1. Ambiguity, cultural differences, mixed messages, social awkwardness and conflict.

2. "Thumbs-up" means praising someone in China while it means asking for a free ride in USA.

Chapter Two Intercultural Communication

I. Decide whether the following statements are true (T) or false (F).

1. F 2. F 3. T 4. T 5. F 6. T 7. T 8. F 9. T 10. T 11. F 12. T 13. T 14. F 15. T 16. T 17. T 18. F 19. T 20. T

II. Discuss the following questions.

1. Theoretically, intercultural communication refers to communication between people whose cultural backgrounds are distinct enough to alter their communication. Practically, it means a dynamic process and interaction among the people with different cultural backgrounds.

2. The dissimilarities among different cultures and various individualistic factors, such as attitudes, communication styles, gender and age, class and status, etc.

3. I think if one knows nothing about his/her culture or the culture of others, the misunderstanding in intercultural communication will happen easily. And the awareness of one's own communication style will also influence intercultural communication.

III. Analyze the following cases and answer the questions.

Case one

(Suggested answers)

1. Hong is very warm hearted and eager to show the typical Chinese hospitality to treat her guest, such as arranging everything without consulting him. Although Joe was thankful for the nice arrangement, he felt disappointed and unhappy because he was deprived of his personal time and freedom to do what he really wanted to do during the visit.

2. If I were Joe, I would tell Hong and the Chair of the Department my real intention politely but directly after expressing my gratitude for their hospitality. I think they will

understand.

3. My suggestion is that we try to learn the culture of others before hosting a friend from another culture and more important is that we try to respect their culture when we show ours.

Case two

(Suggested answers)

1. Fan did know that parking was not allowed on that street from 12:00 a.m. which meant 12:00 noon for her Chinese mind, while in the States, it meant 12:00 midnight.

2. He might think a less severe punishment will help Fan remember the cultural difference of time in USA.

3. You had better learn the cultural differences of other countries before going there.

Ⅳ. Extended Reading.

Passage one

(Suggested answers)

1. Effective intercultural communication produces benefits such as employee productivity and proficiency, teamwork, global business edge and effective leadership.

2. With successful intercultural communication, employees understand the influence of culture on people's behavior and communication tendencies. This enhances teamwork, as colleagues respect one another's cultural background, unique talents and capabilities, which is key to the smooth running of business.

Passage two

(Suggested answers)

1. Language differences, body language, level of context, value of time, negative stereotype and prejudice, feelings and emotions.

2. I think feelings and emotions will be a hard barrier to overcome because they are too individual to control in communication.

Chapter Three Daily Verbal Intercultural Communication

Ⅰ. Decide whether the following statements are true (T) or false (F).

1. T 2. F 3. F 4. F 5. F 6. F 7. T 8. F 9. T 10. T 11. F 12. F 13. T 14. F 15. T 16. F 17. F 18. F 19. T 20. F

Ⅱ. Discuss the following questions.

(Suggested answers)

1. Chinese and Westerners show their hospitality differently in many aspects such as in eating, in dishes and in treating people. For example, Chinese hospitality is shown by the number of the dishes offered, as well as by the eagerness to impress the guest with the most expensive and nutritious food whereas Westerners show their hospitality by giving the guests freedom to choose whatever they want to eat.

2. Politeness is regarded as a virtue in Chinese culture, but for Westerners it is not

always considered positively. In order to communicate well with Westerners, Chinese don't have to be polite in some situations, such as no seeing out when guests leave; no stand-up when your leader comes in; and no help for old people.

3. Chinese usually avoid topics relating to very intimate questions about one's family life, topics concerning death, addressing the senior's given name; Westerners avoid personal questions about age, weight, illness, income, property, religion and politics, etc.

III. Analyze the following cases and answer the questions.

Case one

(Suggested answers)

1. In the first situation, the Westerner used his question as an invitation. The girl understood it only as a question. According to the Chinese tradition, the man should have invited her for lunch since their appointment was to have lunch first. In the second situation, the Westerner used his question as a question rather than an invitation. The girl understood it as an invitation. According to the Chinese tradition, the man should have ordered plenty of food for the girl.

2. The same sentence concealed different intentions. People should try to make sense of what it really means.

Case two

(Suggested answers)

1. Guests to a Chinese family will never be allowed to do any housework. This is one of the ways the host and hostess show their hospitality. Even if the guests offer to cook a dish, the host or the hostess should stay around them and offer help whenever possible. It is even harder to imagine that they would let their guests clear the table and do the dishes, though the guests should always volunteer to help. Shao Bin's meal at a British family sets a great contrast to her Chinese experience. This is why Shao Bin got angry.

2. What she should do is to avoid a hasty conclusion. She should first observe the situation without judgment, and then analyze the situation using what she knows about the differences between Chinese and British culture.

IV. Extended Reading.

(Suggested answers)

1. To give a proper gift, one must understand the culture of the receiver.

2. Welcome gifts: Jade or silver bracelet or necklace may be suitable for a new-born baby; toys or stationary for an older child; something practical such as a walking-stick for old people; some fruits would also be good. Taboo gifts: Books would not be welcome in places like Hong Kong or Macao. Umbrellas would not be welcome in most places in China. Clocks would not be welcome either. Avoid buying odd number of gifts.

3. We should present a gift toward the end of the visit, avoiding giving a gift early in a relationship or at any conspicuous moment. It is a mistake to give the same gift to two or more Japanese of unequal rank.

4. Small souvenir-style gifts will always be appreciated. Fine chocolates can also be an appropriate gift when you are invited to a home, or anything that reflects the interests of your friend and is representative of your country.

5. Flowers, a potted plant, or a bottle of wine are good gift choices.

6. Gifts should only be given to the most intimate friends.

Chapter Four Non-verbal Intercultural Communication

I. Decide whether the following statements are true (T) or false (F).

1. T 2. F 3. T 4. F 5. F 6. T 7. F 8. T 9. T 10. T 11. F 12. T 13. F 14. F 15. T 16. F 17. T 18. F 19. T 20. F

II. Discuss the following questions.

(Suggested answers)

1. Nonverbal communication refers to all aspects of a message which are not conveyed by the literal meaning of words. The functions of nonverbal communication could be identified in the following five aspects: repeating, complementing, substituting, regulating and contradicting.

2. Holding up one's thumb; raising one's little finger; touching or pointing to one's own nose with raised forefinger, etc.

3. Silence is an example in voice modulation that indicates cultural divergence. It is interpreted as evidence of passivity, ignorance, apathy or hesitation in the American culture. Americans fail to appreciate Japanese speech habits, which view silence as necessary and desirable. They tend to think that there is no communication in silence. They try to fill in the pause in conversation, which fortunately can be misunderstood as pushy and noisy. To the Japanese, silence is a rich communication style, which they regard as a virtue.

III. Analyze the following cases and answer the questions.

Case One

(Suggested answers)

1. Stretch out one hand with palm up, which means inviting someone to speak in Chinese culture.

2. No People use different gestures to express the same meaning in different cultures, so it is necessary to know the cultural differences to avoid misunderstanding.

Case Two

(Suggested answers)

1. In Latin America, this gesture is considered very obscene, a signal that you are insulting people.

2. He was using the improper gestures and words to people in Latin America due to his ignorance in cultural differences which led to misunderstanding of the local people.

Case Three

(Suggested answers)

1. Peter was always wearing a smile while apologizing for his mistake, which made the General Manager very angry.

2. Peter wanted to express his friendly and sincere apology with smiles, yet it was considered as impolite and insincere in Japanese culture.

IV. Extended Reading.

(Suggested answers)

1. The effective use of immediacy behaviors increases learning in various contexts and at various levels, and leads to better evaluations by students.

2. Teachers who are judged as less immediate are more likely to sit, touch their heads, shake instead of nodding their heads, use sarcasm, avoid eye contact, and use less expressive nonverbal behaviors.

Chapter Five Interpersonal Relationships

I. Decide whether the following statements are true (T) or false (F).

1. T 2. T 3. T 4. F 5. T 6. F 7. T 8. F 9. T 10. F 11. T 12. F 13. T 14. T 15. T 16. F 17. F 18. T 19. F 20. F

II. Discuss the following questions.

(Suggested answers)

1. Men and women end up talking at cross-purpose. Women tend to speak and hear a language of connection and intimacy (close friendship). Men speak and hear a language of status and independence.

2. Currently, China is undergoing a family restructuring process. One generalization is that the typical Chinese family today can be classified as "4-2-1". "4" represents the parents and parents-in-law, "2" represents the husband and wife, and the "1" represents the only child of the couple. The center of the family is on the "1"—the grandchild.

3. Through understanding the differences, I start to realize that American and Chinese interpretations on friendship obligations are quite different. For instance, Chinese expect friendships to be more lasting; Americans expect friends to be independent; Chinese can usually expect more from their friends than Americans can.

III. Analyze the following cases and answer the questions.

Case one

(Suggested answers)

1. No. Probably because I don't own any property so far. But if my future husband or wife would like to do it, I think I will try to understand from his/her perspective and we'll try to reach an agreement eventually.

2. Tom might hold the view that a pre-nuptial agreement might not be the best move that you want to take if you would like a romantic relationship, but it is definitely the most valuable one because a pre-nuptial agreement could protect your own rights and property in the event of a future divorce or an unexpected death. Lili might hold that a pre-nuptial

agreement casts a shadow of distrust from the very beginning. For her a pre-nup is telling each other, "I love you, but I do not trust you."

Case two

(Suggested answers)

1. Many cultural differences exist in family structures and values. In some cultures, the family is the center of life and the main frame of reference for decisions. In other cultures, the family's reputation and honor depend on each person's actions; in other words, individuals can act without permanently affecting the family life. Some cultures value old people, while other cultures look down on them.

2. Family is the center of most traditional Asians' lives. Many people worry about their families' welfare, reputation and honor. Asian families are often extended, including several generations related by blood or marriage living in the same home.

3. While the traditional family structure and values have changed in recent decades, something's never changed. Throughout history, family has been considered to be the base of Chinese society. And although western life styles have been adopted, the traditional family structure and values still hold a prominent position. The elderly are respected and honored, while young children are the focus of the family.

IV. Extended Reading.

(Suggested answers)

1. Cross-gender friendships are friendships between a male and a female. These friendships diminish in late childhood and early adolescence as boys and girls segregate into separate groups for many activities and socializing, reemerge as possibilities in late adolescence, and reach a peak potential in the college years of early adulthood. Later, adults with spouses or partners are less likely to have cross-sex friendships than single people.

2. Men and women report that they get a richer understanding of how the other gender thinks and feels. It seems these friendships fulfill interaction needs not as commonly met in same-gender friendships. Similarly, women reported that they enjoyed the activity-oriented friendships they had with men.

Chapter Six   Naming and Addressing

I. Decide whether the following statements are true (T) or false (F).

1. T 2. T 3. F 4. F 5. T 6. T 7. T 8. T 9. F 10. F 11. T 12. F 13. F 14. F 15. F 16. F 17. F 18. F 19. T 20. T.

II. Discuss the following questions.

(Suggested answers)

1. Yes. My English name is Olive. My English teacher gave me this name and I like it very much as I like olive oil.

2. It is quite so common for Chinese to use position-linked or occupation-linked titles to address people. In more formal situations, the title along with the last name is appropriate.

Generally speaking, many English-speaking people address others by using the first name. This applies not only to people of roughly the same age, but also of different ages. It is not a sign of discreet.

3. It is considered to be polite and respectful to address a Chinese by his/her surname, followed by honorific titles like Xiān Sheng (Sir), Nǚ Shì (Madam) or the job position. Given names are often called between good friends. Xiǎo Jiě nowadays is considered to be an offensive way to address young ladies.

Ⅲ. Analyze the following cases and answer the questions.

Case one

(Suggested answers)

1. The following aspects might cause the possible intercultural misunderstandings: The "complete silence" reflects the Chinese idea of students' appropriate behaviors in class; The Chinese way of addressing a teacher by his/her occupation instead of his/her names is different from the American way; The students' way of asking questions sounds somewhat impolite to the English speakers and the question itself could be considered as a private one; The way the Chinese student gives himself/herself English name might confuse the American teacher (such as the name "Gypsy"); etc..

2. I think she came to China because she was not happy with her job and wanted to get away from it or because she just needed a life change and coming to China seemed to her a solution at that time.

Case two

(Suggested answers)

1. First, the students' way of addressing their teacher by using her occupation indicates their respect to the teacher. Second, students adopt the Chinese way of naming to make their English names. Both are not considered as appropriate in the English speaking context.

2. I'll try to explain that Chinese names can give all sorts of information about a person. They may give clues about where and when the person was born. Or they may tell us something about family relationships, ethnic group, parents' expectation for the children, sex (though nowadays it is more difficult to tell a girl's name from a boy's), values or even personal characteristics. I will also tell him/her that although some students know that naming can be different in other cultures, they tend to adopt their native way while choosing their English names.

Ⅳ. Extended Reading.

(Suggested answers)

1. I think I feel a little awkward when people around start to use these terms more often than before. I guess it's because the more eager people try to instantly create a connection with me, the more I start to feel alienated to them. But I don't see it as being offended.

2. 师傅 (shīfu) and 老师 (lǎoshī) are the two other terms that I could think of. Traditionally 师傅 (shīfu) is a title for a skilled worker, now still quite commonly used to

any unknown ordinary people of both sexes, usually middle-aged or older persons, especially those who provide services. 老师 (lǎoshī) is a respectful term of address to a learned or professional person, who is not necessarily a teacher, used to either male or female, if to a known person, often used with the surname, commonly used.

3. (open answer)

Chapter Seven　Culturally-loaded Words in Communication

Ⅰ. Decide whether the following statements are true (T) or false (F).

1. F　2. F　3. T　4. T　5. T　6. T　7. F　8. F　9. F　10. T　11. F　12. F　13. T　14. F　15. F　16. F　17. T　18. T　19. T　20. T

Ⅱ. Give the Chinese equivalents of the following proverbs and idioms.

1. 天网恢恢疏而不漏。
2. 精明鬼遇上精明鬼。
3. 金玉良言。
4. 肥缺,肥差。
5. 船到桥头自然直。
6. 宁做鸡头不做凤尾。
7. 牛饮/酒量大如海。
8. 如履薄冰。

Ⅲ. Translate the following statements. Pay attention to the number words.

1. 七横八竖,乱七八糟
2. 考虑再三
3. 三三两两地
4. 两人智慧胜一人;人多好办事;三个臭皮匠顶个诸葛亮
5. ——能便宜一点吗?
   ——对不起,一口价。
6. ——你今晚约 Pam 出去吗?
   ——这问题太难回答!
7. 他只喝了半瓶酒,就有了三分醉意。
8. 十之八九他会忘记。(表示很有可能)

Ⅳ. Analyze the following cases and answer the questions.

Case one

(Suggested answers)

1. In China "wearing a green hat" (戴绿帽子 or dài lǜ mào zi) is an expression that Chinese use when a woman cheats on her husband or boyfriend because the phrase sounds similar to the word for "cuckold". This apparently dates back to the Yuan Dynasty when the relatives of prostitutes were forced to wear green hats.

2. A white elephant is a possession which its owner cannot dispose of and whose cost, particularly that of maintenance, is out of proportion to its usefulness.

Case two
(Suggested answers)

1. Number 13 is a troubling number in many Western countries, so in daily life, people avoid number 13. For example, they avoid eating with 13 people sitting together or serving 13 dishes. House, floor and various serial numbers also try to avoid "13". For when Jesus and his disciples were having dinner, the thirteenth people was Judah who betrayed Jesus for 30 silver coins, then Jesus was crucified in the 13th on Friday.

2. The number 8 is considered to be auspicious in Chinese culture. Because 8 has the similar pronunciation with 发 (fā, meaning wealth or fortune), this number is very welcome among Chinese people. The popularity of 8 was obvious in relation to the Beijing Olympic Games which commenced at exactly eight o'clock eight minutes on the eighth day of the eighth month in 2008. When people choose telephone numbers, mobile numbers, house numbers, car identification numbers and important dates, 8 is usually the first choice.

Ⅴ. **Extended Reading.**
Passage one
(Suggested answers)

1. The following are the examples the passage touches upon on color psychology: Red or orange pills are generally used as stimulants; The company Glasgow installed blue street lights in certain neighborhoods which resulted in a reduced crime rate; Males reported that red colored outfits made women seem more attractive, while women answered that the color of a male's outfit did not affect his attractiveness; The color pink is heavily used on Victoria's Secret branding; Warm colors tended to attract spontaneous purchasers, despite cooler colors being more favorable.

2. I'd like to talk about that not only culture, but gender can also influence how an individual perceives color. I noticed that in most cases the colors of babies' clothes are gender-segregated: pink and red are often for baby girls while blue and green are for baby boys. It seems that this doesn't have much to do with culture differences.

Passage two
(Suggested answers)

1. I think though it is mostly subconscious, colors do affect people's mood in different ways, which explains why in both Chinese and English there are many words or expressions with color to describe people's feelings, such as "see red", or "吓得脸色发白".

2. I believe that one's feelings about color are often deeply personal and rooted in one's own experience or culture. While perceptions of color are somewhat subjective, there are some color effects that have universal meaning. For example, the color red is known as a warm color which is said to evoke emotions ranging from feelings of warmth and comfort to feelings of anger and hostility.

Chapter Eight Intercultural Communication Competence

Ⅰ. **Decide whether the following statements are true (T) or false (F).**

1. F 2. T 3. T 4. F 5. T 6. F 7. F 8. F 9. F 10. F 11. T 12. T 13. F 14. F 15. T 16. T 17. F 18. T 19. F 20. T

Ⅱ. **Discuss the following questions.**

(Suggested answers)

1. To compare the similarities and differences of different cultural backgrounds, scholars have proposed different frames of cultural comparison. In this chaper, two classifications developed by Kluchhohn and Hofstede respectively are introduced. They will help us have a deeper understanding of different cultures and become better intercultural communicators.

2. Culture shock can be described as the feeling of confusion and disorientation that one experiences when facing with a large number of new and unfamiliar people and situations. To avoid it, first, one needs to be aware that everyone experiences some degree of culture shock when entering a new culture for some length of time. Second, one is suggested to study the host culture and the local environment, learn basic verbal and nonverbal language skills, develop intercultural relationships, maintain an intimate social network, assume the principle of difference, and anticipate future events, etc..

3. Intercultural communication competence refers to the ability to accomplish effective and appropriate intercultural communication between communicators of different cultures. In short, it is often written as "ICC". There are some suggestions on how to improve one's ICC: control the effects of criticism of the new culture as well as negative attitudes towards the new culture; develop cognitive complexity (which refers to the ability of a person to perceive a wide variety of things about another person and culture); foster one's confidence and self-esteem; be eager to experiment with new approaches and especially a willingness to learn; trust in people; have the desire to learn the language, to become knowledgeable about the culture, and to adapt to a new culture; etc..

Ⅲ. **Analyze the following cases and answer the questions.**

Case one

(Suggested answers)

1. Because he is experiencing the feeling of confusion and disorientation facing with the large number of new and unfamiliar people and situations in China. One may call it a culture shock.

2. Yes, it is. Everyone experiences some degree of culture shock when entering a new culture for some length of time.

3. I don't think his reaction is suitable. If I experience such situations, I would try not to reject the environment; Instead, I would develop friendship with some local people, talk to my relatives, learn the new culture, or just listen to my favorite music while doing

exercises. I'm convinced that the negative feelings and frustration will fade away eventually.

Case two

(Suggested answers)

(6) A kind of cultural integration is reflected in this case. That is, Chinese culture is integrated with American culture as melting pot.

(7) The ancient city of Chang'an in the Tang Dynasty, Vancouver in Canada, etc..

Case three

(Suggested answer)

From this passage, we find that people's attitudes towards silence and modesty, gifting etiquettes, and liberation of women in society can also serve as clues to help understand intercultural communication.

Ⅳ. Extended Reading.

(Suggested answers)

Developing cross-cultural competence would enable individuals to adapt effectively in intercultural environments and help them communicate their point of view to an audience belonging to a different cultural ethnicity and background.

Bibliography

[1] Anderson Peter. Explaining Intercultural Differences in nonverbal Communication// Samovar L A, Porter R E. Intercultural communication: A Reader. Belmont, Calif.: Wadsworth Publishing Co, 1988.

[2] Blanton L L, Linda Lee. The Multicultural Workshop. Beijing: China Machine Press, 1999.

[3] Brick J. China: A Handbook in Intercultural Communication. Sydney: the National Center for English Language Teaching and Research, 1991.

[4] Brislin Richard, Tomoko Yoshida. Intercultural Communication Training: An Introduction. Thousand Oaks, Calif.: Sage Publications, Inc, 1994.

[5] Dai Fan, Stephen L J Smith. Cultures in Contrast: Miscommunication and Misunderstandings between Chinese and North Americans. Shanghai: Shanghai Foreign Education Press, 2003.

[6] Dodd Carley H. Dynamics of Intercultural Communications. Shanghai: Shanghai Foreign Language Education Press, 2007.

[7] Don Snow. Encounters with Westerners: Improving Skills in English and Intercultural Communication. Shanghai: Shanghai Foreign Language Education Press, 2004.

[8] Gudykunst William B, Yong Yun Kim. Communicating with Strangers: An Approach to Intercultural Communication. 5th ed. Shanghai: Shanghai Foreign Language Education Press, 2007.

[9] Hall Edward. The Silent Language. New York: Doubleday and Company, 1959.

[10] Hall Edward. Monochromic and Polychromic Time. The Dance of Life: The Other Dimension of Time. New York: Doubleday and Company, 1983.

[11] Hoopes D S. Readings in Intercultural Communication: Vol. II. La Grange Park, Illinois: Intercultural Network, Inc, 1977.

[12] Kim Y Y, Gudykunst W B. Theories in Intercultural Communication. Beverly Hills, Calif.: Sage Publications, Inc, 1984.

[13] Lustig Myron W, Jolene Koester. Intercultural Competence: Interpersonal Communication Across Cultures. 5th ed. Shanghai: Shanghai Foreign Language Education Press, 2007.

[14] Martin Judith N, Thomas K Nakayama. Intercultural Communication in Contexts.

3rd ed. New York：McGraw-Hill Companies，Inc，2004.

[15] Oatey Helen. Chinese and Western Interpersonal Relationships//Hu Wenzhong. Intercultural Communication-What It Means to Chinese Learners of English. Shanghai：Shanghai Translation Publishing House，1988：45 - 47.

[16] Ouyang Fasu. Some Typical Cultural Mistakes Made by Chinese Learners of English//Hu Wenzhong. Intercultural Communication-What It Means to Chinese Learners of English. Shanghai：Shanghai Translation Publishing House，1988：50 - 52.

[17] Paulston C B. Linguistic Interaction, Intercultural Communication and Communicative Language Teaching//Hu Wenzhong. Intercultural Communication-What It Means to Chinese Learners of English. Shanghai：Shanghai Translation Publishing House，1988：58 - 60.

[18] Saee John. Managing Organization in a Global Economy (An Intercultural Perspective). Mason, Ohio：South-Western, part of the Thomson Corporation, 2005.

[19] Samovar Larry A, Richard E Porter, Lisa A Stefani. Communication between Cultures. Beijing：Foreign Language Teaching and Research Press，2007.

[20] Samovar Larry A, Porter R E. Intercultural Communication：A Reader. Belmont, Calif.：Wadsworth Publishing Co.

[21] Scollon R, Scollon S W. Intercultural Communication：A Discourse Approach. Cambridge, Mass.：Blackwell Publishers Inc，1995.

[22] Seelye H N. Teaching Culture：Strategies for Intercultural Communication. Lincolnwood，Illinois：National Textbook Company，1993.

[23] 毕继万. 跨文化非语言交际. 北京：高等教育出版社，2009.

[24] 布罗斯纳安，毕继万. 中国和英语国家非语言交际对比. 北京：北京语言学院出版社，1991.

[25] 戴凡，Stephen L J Smith. 文化碰撞：中国北美人际交往误解剖析. 上海：上海外语教育出版社，2003.

[26] 丁启红. 委婉语与禁忌语对比研究. 成都：成都理工大学，2006.

[27] 窦卫霖. 跨文化交际基础. 北京：对外经济贸易大学出版社，2007.

[28] 杜学增. 中英文化习俗比较. 北京：外语教学与研究出版社，1999.

[29] 关世杰. 跨文化交流学——提高涉外交流能力的学问. 北京：北京大学出版社，1995.

[30] 何维湘. 跨文化交际技巧. 广州：中山大学出版社，2004.

[31] 胡超. 跨文化交际实用教程. 北京：学与研究出版社，2006.

[32] 胡文仲. 跨文化交际面面观. 北京：北京大学出版社，1999.

[33] 贾玉新. 跨文化交际学. 上海：上海外语教育出版社，1997.

[34] 林大津. 跨文化交际研究. 福州：福建人民出版社，2008.

[35] 刘凤霞. 跨文化交际教程. 北京：北京大学出版社，2005.

[36] 王宗炎. 自我认识与跨文化交际. 上海：上海外语教育出版社，1996.

[37] 许力生. 跨文化交际英语教程. 上海：上海外语教育出版社，2004.
[38] 徐行言. 中西文化比较. 北京：北京大学出版社，2004.
[39] 严明. 大学英语跨文化交际教程. 北京：清华大学出版社，2009.
[40] 乐黛云. 跨文化之桥. 北京：北京大学出版社，2002.
[41] 张爱琳. 跨文化交际. 重庆：重庆大学出版社，2007.
[42] 张蓓. 郑文园. 跨文化意识. 北京：清华大学出版社，2003.
[43] 赵毅. 钱为钢. 言语交际. 上海：上海文艺出版社，2000.
[44] 郑晓泉. 跨文化交际. 杭州：浙江大学出版社，2010.